ETHNIC DRINKING SUBCULTURES

ANDREW M. GREELEY

WILLIAM C. McCREADY

GARY THEISEN

*Center for the Study of American Pluralism,
National Opinion Research Center*

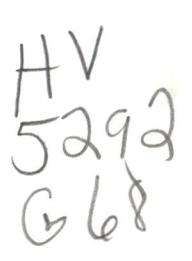

PRAEGER

PRAEGER SPECIAL STUDIES • PRAEGER SCIENTIFIC
A J.F. BERGIN PUBLISHERS BOOK

Library of Congress Cataloging in Publication Data
Greeley, Andrew M   1928-
   Ethnic Drinking Subcultures.

   "A J.F. Bergin Publishers Book."
   Bibliography; p. 138
   Includes Index.
   1. Minorities   United States   Alcohol use.
   I. McCready, William C., 1941- joint author.
   II. Theisen, Gary, joint author. III. Title.
   HV5292.G68   394.1'3'0973   79-13904
   ISBN 0-03-052731-7

Published in 1980 by Praeger Publishers
CBS Educational and Professional Publishing
A Division of CBS, Inc.
521 Fifth Avenue, New York, New York 10017, U.S.A.

© 1980 by J.F. Bergin Publishers, Inc.

All rights reserved
J.F. Bergin Publishers, Inc.
One Hanson Place
Brooklyn, New York 11243

0123456789   056   987654321

Printed in the United States of America

Composition by TYPECON

Research reported here was supported in part by a grant from the Extra-Mural Research Branch of the National Institute on Alcohol Abuse and Alcoholism

CONTENTS

1	Ethnicity and Alcohol	1
2	Approaches to Ethnicity	15
3	Drinking Subcultures	36
4	Explaining Drinking Subcultures	53
5	Socialization Subcultures	71
6	Drug Usage and Drinking Among Ethnic Groups	83
7	Drinking Subcultures and Assimilation	89
8	Conclusion	95
Appendix A	Data Collection Methodology	101
Appendix B	Comparison of Respondents and Non-respondents: The Refused Interviews	111
Appendix C	Questionnaire Items Used to Construct Variables	121
Appendix D	A Modest Attempt at Self-Validation	127
Bibliography		131
Index		135

ETHNIC DRINKING SUBCULTURES

CHAPTER ONE
Ethnicity and Alcohol

This book is about three subjects: alcohol consumption, ethnic diversity, and socialization. It will investigate the drinking behavior of major ethnic groups in the United States and how these groups socialize their offspring in drinking behavior patterns. In the process of studying different "drinking subcultures"—patterns of attitudes and behaviors toward the use of alcoholic beverages—we shall also learn about the dynamics of ethnic diversity in the United States and how ethnic subcultures, which are part of the national culture yet in some ways distinct from it, manage to persist.

In this first chapter we will discuss differences in ethnic drinking and, in the next chapter, turn to a theoretical consideration of ethnic subcultures which will provide a framework for the analysis to be reported in the following chapters. We will defer to the final chapter wide-ranging speculation about the role of ethnicity in American life and its importance as a social problem and in social-policy areas like alcohol use and abuse.

Drinking is increasing in the United States. In a January 1976 Gallup Poll, 66 percent of the women and 77 percent of the men said they drink. The national average is 71 percent, the highest proportion of drinkers in the United States since Gallup began monitoring drinking behavior in 1939. Problem drinking has also increased: in 1966 12 percent of the Gallup families said that liquor has an adverse effect on their family life, while a decade later the proportion rose to 18 percent of those who answered yes to the question, "Has liquor ever been a cause of trouble in your family?" One estimate is that the U.S. economy loses close to 70 million dollars each day because of alcoholism or problem drinking.

Drinking also seems to be increasing among adolescents. In the early 1960s, only half the teenagers in the country consumed alcohol. The proportion now is 70 percent. More than 25 percent drink in cars at night; more than one-third are intoxicated once a month; more than 90 percent of the high school seniors in the country have used alcohol, while only little more than one-third have used marijuana.

Drinking, then, is widespread among American adults and adolescents, and drinking problems seem to be increasing in both generations. There are, however, rather striking differences between various groups of Americans in their drinking behavior. Eighty-two percent of the college-educated individuals in the country drink, as opposed to 71 percent of those who have a high school education; 81 percent of Roman Catholics drink, as opposed to 64 percent of Protestants; 79 percent of those who live in the eastern portion of the country drink, as opposed to 57 percent of those who live in the South.

The study reported here focuses on one of the most striking varieties of drinking behavior that can be found in American society—the differences between certain religious and ethnic groups.

THE FACT OF ETHNIC DIFFERENCE

Alcoholism research is one of the few areas in American social science that never lost interest in ethnic diversity. As far back as 1946 and 1947, Bales (1946) and Glad (1947) noted the differences between Irish and Jewish drinking behavior. In the late 1950s, Snyder (1958) intensively studied the differences between Jewish and Catholic drinking patterns. Earlier, Strauss and Bacon (1951) reported the differences in drinking habits between Jewish and Irish college students. McCord and McCord (1960) confirmed the finding of high Irish alcoholism rates in longitudinal research with a small and unrepresentative sample (38 percent of young Irish men in the sample became alcoholics as opposed to 6 percent of the Italians). Skolnick (1954) repeated the finding in a study of arrests for inebriety. Lolli and his colleagues (1958), studying drinking patterns in both Italian and French cultures in the Old World, confirmed that at least for the Italians moderation in drink was rooted in cultural heritage. More recently, Knupfer and Room (1967) replicated the finding of ethnic diversity in their study in Oakland, California, and Henry Wechsler and his colleagues (1968) found once again that the Irish had a high incidence of drinking problems and that that of Jews and Italians was low. Others who have focused on ethnic characteristics in drinking behavior are Roberts and Meyers (1958), Ober and Singer (1961), Jellinek (1960), Ullman (1958), and Bacon and Jones (1968).

There are few findings in social science so often repeated. Irish tend to have a serious problem with drinking; Jews and Italians do not. There is, however, relatively little national-survey data to confirm this finding. Most of the studies noted are based on small, nonrandom, local samples. Cahalan, Cisin, and Crossley (1969) have done several tables based on father's country of origin which show Irish to be less likely to be heavy drinkers than either Italians or those of English background, though they are more likely to be heavy drinkers than Jews. In actuality, however, since the authors look only at the children of foreign-born parents, they leave out substantial numbers of the early immigrant groups, particulary the Irish. National-survey data collected by National Opinion Research Center,

(NORC) in the middle 1960s (1966) does conform to predicted ethnic differences (See Table 1.1).*

Of all American groups, the Irish are the least likely to be "nonabstainers," the most likely to report drinking twice a week or more, and the most likely to consume three or more drinks of hard liquor at a sitting (Tables 1.2 and 1.3). The Slavic group edges out the Irish in the proportion who use drink to enhance enjoyment (Table 1.4). But the Irish lag behind U.S. Protestants and are only slightly ahead of Slavs and German Catholics on the scale of serious drink problems (Table 1.5). Finally, on a scale measuring incipient alcoholism, Irish drinkers are behind both English and Slavs but are ahead of other U.S. ethnic groups (Table 1.6). In terms of absolute proportions, then, more Irish are problem drinkers than are the English. Since Tables 1.2 through 1.6 deal only with those who drink, the data show that the English who do drink have drinking problems as much as those of the Irish. Since the English are much less likely to drink (by some 30 percent), in absolute terms they have fewer problems.

The NORC data suggests that *among drinkers* the Irish are no more likely to have a serious alcohol problem than are many other groups in U.S. society. It just so happens that accidents of geography juxtaposed the Irish in early research with groups that have phenomenally low drinking problems.** The pertinent question for the Irish is not why they become alcoholics or problem drinkers but why they drink and why they drink so much.

There is less evidence on the continuation of drinking patterns in younger generations. Straus and Bacon (1951) studied college students, but those were students of two decades ago; McCord and McCord (1960) also reported on young people growing up in the late 1930s and 1940s Knupfer and Room (1967) reported a notable increase in drinking among Jews under 40 but found no relationship between drinking and how long one's family had been in the country, suggesting that drinking patterns among ethnic groups have a remarkable persistence over time.

In summary, then, there is overwhelming evidence of differences among American ethnic groups and drinking patterns, particularly among Italians, Jews, and Irish. There seems to be some reason for expecting these differences to persist from generation to generation. There is also, however, evidence that among drinkers the incidence of alcoholism among the Irish is not abnormally high, but rather that among the Italians and Jews the incidence is abnormally low.

*Tables and Figures follow the text of the chapter in which they are first cited.
**The Italians, the Jews, and the Irish were the ethnic groups most likely to be studied because they were the ones closest to the universities where the studies were being done, particularly Yale and Rutgers. One had to go only just beyond the walls of these universities to find large segments of all three communities.

ETHNICITY AND ALCOHOL: EXPLANATIONS

Broadly speaking, there are two types of psychosocial explanations to be found for alcoholism—cultural, and psychological.* The cultural approach to alcoholism is evident in the study of France and Italy previously cited and in various studies of Japanese, Mexican, Nigerian, Indian, Australian, and English drinking patterns. This literature stresses the social meaning and the social function of drinking and drunkenness and describes how different patterns of alcohol use have emerged in different societies.

The psychological literature is immense and includes both a personality measurement and a psychoanalytic component. It is said that the potential alcoholic comes from a stressful, anxiety-producing family background, and possesses a weak ego and a confused self-image. His or her dependency needs are strong and there may be a strain of latent homosexuality. Socially maladjusted, depressed, and unable to relate, the potential alcoholic has, not unexpectedly, poor morale. Recently McClellan has reinterpreted drinking behavior as an assertion of male "power drive" (1972). He sees drinking resulting *not* from a dependency need and a desire for oral gratification (as does the psychoanalytic literature) but rather from the lack of outlets for socialized power. In a culture in which the demands for male supportiveness are high and there is low support for assertiveness in the male role, McClellan argues, drinking increases in men at least, the personalized power fantasies that are an escape from frustration.

Neither the cultural nor the personality explanation of alcoholism claims to be exclusive. It is still true, however, that there tends to be an emphasis in most work either on the family-structure personality explanation or on the sociocultural explanation. It is our intention to attempt to integrate the two explanations around a model that emphasizes the family as a socialization agency.

Why are the Irish far more likely than the Italians and the Jews to have serious drinking problems? If you lean to a cultural explanation, you may agree with Glad that:

> It was found that the Jews tend to regard the function of drinking as (a) socially practical and (b) religiously symbolic and communicative. The common element in these two uses lies in their instrumentality to

---

*Joyce Fitzpatrick O'Connor, in an unpublished study of drinking patterns in Ireland and England, suggests as a third explanation a social-structural perspective. According to Ms. O'Connor (personal communication), the weight of her evidence links the high levels of drinking among Irish to the fact that there are no recreational institutions available for large numbers of young people in the countryside other than the local public house. In a country which until recently was both depressed and oppressed, the public house was the only recreational institution that ordinary people could sustain.

the attainment of goals remote from the effects of alcoholism per se. The Irish tend to regard the functions of drinking as (a) promotion of fun and pleasure and (b) conviviality. Both of these define the purpose of drinking in terms of effective consequences, in which the physiological and psychological changes produced in the individual by alcohol per se are of primary importance (1947).

According to Bales (1946) and Snyder (1958), Jewish culture has been able to integrate drinking into a religious and symbolic context in which there are very powerful cultural norms both for the respect of alcohol and against the imitation of Gentile drunkenness. Irish culture, on the other hand, has not been able to develop such norms; among the Irish there is virtually no ritual drinking in the religious sense. For Jews drinking tends to be ritual; for the Irish it is convivial or even utilitarian—a way of dispelling grief, releasing sexual and aggressive tension, gaining advantage over others. Alcoholic drinks, according to Bacon and Jones (1968), have served among the Irish as a substitute for food both physically and psychologically: "Drink alone serves as a symbol for hospitality for the Irish, but for many other people—again the Jews are a good example—food and drink together serve this function" (1968:126).

The Italians, unlike the Irish and like the Jews, have been able to integrate drinking into a stable life pattern. The Italian pattern reflects a long tradition of drinking wine in a leisurely family mealtime gathering; drinking is seen simply as one aspect of a pleasurable daily event. Unlike the Irish child, the Italian child is introduced to alcohol at an early age at home: "Single experiences with too much drink often happened early in life, within the family group, and were generally accepted as a matter of course as the side effects of growing up—much like a childhood stomach-ache from too much candy (1968:182)."

Italian culture has been able to integrate drinking as secular behavior related to food consumption. Alcohol is a kind of food and consumption of it is as natural and unthreatening as eating a meal. Jewish culture has, in addition, been able to achieve a religious integration of drink. "Drinking has a very special significance in Jewish ritual, and it is in religious terms that young people usually first experience alcohol... wine represents a whole network of sacred things" (1968:162). The Irish, on the other hand, have achieved neither religious nor secular integration and hence are much more prone to drink to escape problems.

If, on the other hand, one stresses the psychological study of alcoholism, one will search in the patterns of Irish family life for an explanation in the strong, domineering mother, the weak, overwhelmed father (at least in urban Irish life), sexual puritanism, a lack of explicit affection, the coldness and rigidity of Irish Catholicism, the weak self-concept resulting from the stern social control (enforced particularly by ridicule) during the childhood years, and the resulting erratic and anxiety-ridden personality. All of these may explain why the Irish personality seems prone to seek escape from tensions and anxieties in the heavy consumption of alcohol.

There are obvious weaknesses in both explanations. Hoffman, Loper, and Kanmeier (1974) found little success in identifying future alcoholics with Minnesota Multiphasic Personality Inventory (MMPI) scales. There did not seem to be much in the way of personality differences between prealcoholics and others. (There are differences, of course, between actual alcoholics and nonalcoholics on personality scales, but scale scores taken early in life do not predict later alcoholic behavior). Knupfer and Room (1967), citing the Manhattan Mental Health Study, point out that there is little difference in tension and anxiety between Irish and Jews. Patterns of heavy alcohol consumption in Ireland apparently go back to pre-Christian times and certainly antedate sexual puritanism, which Larkin (1972) and Kennedy (1973) have demonstrated are mid-nineteenth-century phenomena. Furthermore, current studies of drinking behavior in Ireland itself suggest that alcoholism is no more a serious problem than it is in other North Atlantic countries and may be substantially less a problem there than in either England or the United States. Stivers (1976) suggests that to the extent there is a drinking problem in Ireland it is the result of the collapse of the traditional Irish culture under the impact of the famine of the middle of the last century: "The traditional roles of landowner, husband, father, prior sources of male identity, were devalued at the expense of the roles of the hard drinker, athlete, and conversationalist.... Hard drinking was a means of establishing and sustaining one's status in the bachelor group. It was a prerequisite for membership" (1976:67). Nor do the explanations offered by either the psychological or cultural "schools" explain why among drinkers the Irish are no more likely to be alcoholics than are members of many other American ethnic groups, including the English Protestant group. What has to be explained is not why the Irish are more likely to be alcoholics but why the Italians and the Jews are less likely to be alcoholics than members of most other American religioethnic communities.

We hope to resolve the problem of the two explanations by testing a model which assumes that the Irish (for example) drink more than others because they grow up in Irish families and live in Irish environs.* The

---

*A sense of justice moves the authors to note that whatever is to be said about the drinking of Irish Americans, the Irish Irish are not, contrary to popular impression, the world's heaviest drinkers. Per capita alcohol consumption in the republic is twenty-third in a list of the world's nations (nineteenth for consumption of spirits). Of the nine EEC countries, Ireland was eighth in the per capita consumption of alcohol and sixth in the per capita consumption of spirits. However, the per capita sum spent on drink in Ireland (between 11 percent and 14 percent per year during the 1970s is the highest in the EEC—mostly because of very high government taxes (Cowley 1978).

question, then, becomes one of how drinking socialization takes place in a family context and how important imitation, cultural norm transmission, and family structure are.

TABLE 1.1*

RANK ORDER OF AMERICAN WHITE ETHNIC GROUPS
ON PROPORTION OF "NONABSTAINERS"

"Do you ever have occasion to use alcoholic beverages such as liquor, wine, or beer, or are you a total abstainer?"

	Percentage of "nonabstainers"
Irish	92
Jewish	90
German Catholic	89
Slavic	88
Italian	88
Scandinavian	77
German Protestant	70
WASP	63

*Tables 1.1 through 1.6 are all from _The Education of Catholic Americans_, NORC, 1966.

TABLE 1.2

RANK ORDER OF AMERICAN WHITE ETHNIC GROUPS
ON PROPORTION OF DRINKING TWICE A WEEK
OR MORE (OF THOSE WHO DRINK)

"How often during the last year did you have one or more drinks?"

	Percentage drinking twice a week or more
Irish	42
Slavic	29
German Catholic	28
WASP	24
Scandinavian	22
German Prtotestant	21
Italian	15
Jewish	15

TABLE 1.3

RANK ORDER OF AMERICAN WHITE ETHNIC GROUPS
ON PROPORTION OF CONSUMING THREE OR MORE
DRINKS OF HARD LIQUOR AT A SITTING

"How many drinks of liquor (whiskey, gin, vodka, etc.) do you consume at a sitting?"

	Percentage of three or more
Irish	33
German Catholic	26
WASP	24
German Protestant	21
Slavic	20
Italian	16
Jewish	11

TABLE 1.4

RANK ORDER AMONG AMERICAN WHITE ETHNIC GROUPS
ON THE USE OF DRINK AS AN ENJOYMENT

"Alcoholic beverages
    make a social gathering more enjoyable
    are customary on special occasions
    help me enjoy a party
    make me more carefree"

Slavic	2.22
Irish	2.15
German Catholic	1.96
Jewish	1.94
Italian	1.75
German Protestant	1.39
Scandinavian	1.33
WASP	1.26

TABLE 1.5

RANK ORDER OF AMERICAN WHITE ETHNIC GROUPS
ON SERIOUS DRINK PROBLEM*

Items:**
  I neglect my regular meals when I am drinking.
  Liquor has less effect on me than it used to.
  I awaken next day not being able to remember some
    of the things I had done while I was drinking.
  I don't nurse my drinks; I toss them down pretty fast.
  I stay intoxicated for several days at a time.
  Once I start drinking it is difficult for me to
    stop before I become completely intoxicated.
  Without realizing what I am doing, I end up drinking
    more than I had planned to.

WASP	1.56
Irish	1.37
German Catholic	1.36
Slavic	1.32
German Protestant	1.25
Scandinavian	1.16
Jewish	.68
Italian	.55

* In this and subsequent tables both male and female respondents are included and there is no standardization for social class.

** A response of "Frequently" was scored 3.

TABLE 1.6

RANK ORDER AMONG AMERICAN WHITE ETHNIC GROUPS
ON HAVING MAJOR TROUBLE WITH DRINKING

Items:
  Has an employer ever fired or threatened to fire you if you did not cut down or quit drinking?
  Has your spouse ever left you or threatened to leave you if you didn't do something about your drinking?
  Has your spouse ever complained that you spend too much money on alcoholic beverages?
  Have you ever been picked up or arrested by the police for intoxication or other charges involving alcoholic beverages?
  Has a physician ever told you that drinking was injuring your health?

Slavic	.750
WASP	.295
Irish	.294
German Catholic	.277
Scandinavian	.217
Italian	.214
Jewish	.183
German Protestant	.175

CHAPTER TWO
Approaches to Ethnicity

One can identify at least six different approaches to the study of ethnic diversity in the United States.

1. *Ideological.* The primary question of this approach is whether ethnicity is "a good thing." Should one even study it, since by studying it one tends to encourage it? In a rationalistic, universalistic society, distinctions based on origin are reactionary, regressive, chauvinistic, and even fascistic. Orlando Patterson (1978) and Stein and Hill (1970), are the most articulate proponents of the position that ethnicity should not be even named among us *(ne nominatur inter vos).* On the other hand, ethnic writers such as Richard Gambino (1974) and Michael Novak (1971) have argued against Anglo-Saxon Protestant (and Irish Catholic) oppression of ethnics and ethnic subcultural preferences in the United States. The former are horrified by ethnic diversity, the latter glory in it; neither side of this particular debate is notably encumbered by empirical evidence.

2. *Identity and identification.* The principal question in this approach focuses on the role of ethnicity in contemporary industrial society. It is most elegantly stated by Harold Isaacs (1975) and Donald Horowitz (1975). This approach explains the persistence of ethnicity as the result of a search for "basic group identity," "self-definition," or "social location." People identify with their ethnic group so that they will know who they are in the midst of a society that is for the most part formal, bureaucratic, and ascriptive. Some empirical research has been done from this perspective, seeking to determine how important ethnic identification is as a means of self-definition in the contemporary United States and to what extent ethnic customs and practices that reinforce that self-definition are still important to Americans.

3. *Acculturation and assimilation.* Milton Gordon (1964) introduced these terms into the discussion. Acculturation for Gordon consists of the immigrant group's taking on the behavior patterns of the host society; assimilation consists of the immigrant group losing its concern about maintaining its most intimate relationships (marriage and friendship) within the group boundaries. Gordon has suggested that in the United States assimilation proceeds at a much slower rate than acculturation. Those who are influenced by Gordon's approach attempt to define

15

measures of assimilation and acculturation and compare progress on both (1975). Thus, Alba (1975) has studied the increasing rates of ethnic exogamy and concluded that ethnicity is declining rapidly as an important factor in American life.

4. *Conflict.* This approach focuses on ethnic diversity as the axis of political competition and conflict in the industrial world. Glazer and Moynihan (1970) suggest that the ethnic collectivities in New York City are no longer bearers of separate cultural systems, but are rather political interest groups. Much of the analysis done by political scientists and anthropologists in Third World countries emphasizes conflict among various ethnic groups. Separate 1975 articles by Kilson, Porter, das Gupta, Esman, and Mazuri, for example, discuss the various aspects of ethnic or racial-ethnic conflict in different nations. The primary question in this approach is which group dominates, what groups are dominated, and how the patterns of dominance and subservience are worked out. While such writers as Patterson, Stein, Hill and, to some extent, Isaacs are concerned about the dangers in ethnic conflict, scholars using the conflict model of ethnicity typically assume that conflict is a given and try to determine who is conflicting with whom.

5. *Social class.* Early in the revival of interest in ethnic identity there were efforts by a number of writers—most notably Herbert Gans (1962)—to equate ethnicity with social class. More recently others have suggested that while ethnicity is not the same as class, ethnic stratification is a variety of class stratification. Just as humans can be stratified according to education, income, and social prestige, they can also be stratified as to whether they have membership in more prestigious or less prestigious ethnic groups. The primary question for those who use this research model concerns what the ethnic prestige ranking is and how that prestige ranking came to be.

6. *Subcultural persistence.* This approach, which has characterized much of the research done at the Center for the Study of American Pluralism at NORC, is concerned primarily with the persistence of ethnically linked attitudes and behaviors regardless of such assimilationist influences and degree of ethnic self-identification.

Perhaps it does not need to be observed that none of the six approaches is necessarily incompatible. Although Orlando Patterson maintains that ethnicity should not be discussed, he is nevertheless prepared to discuss it and, once one concedes that ethnicity may be discussed, then issues of self-definition, acculturation, conflict, stratification, and subcultural persistence become pertinent. Those of us who focus on subcultural persistence, however, believe that our investigations begin where the other five approaches end. We have found that the persistence of some subcultural traits seem relatively independent of self-definition, are unaffected by acculturation and social class, and have nothing to do with political competition and conflict. In *Ethnicity in the United States* (1964) and "The Transmission of Cultural Heritage: The Case of the Irish and the Italians" (1975), we report that hypotheses fashioned from a knowledge of the Old World cultural heritages of immigrant groups are quite likely to be sustained when examined against data on attitudes and behaviors of the ethnic groups that have emerged from emigration from their old societies. If we know, for example, how the Irish and the Italians behaved in the old countries, we can be successful most of the time in predicting differences between them in the United States. Thus, we conclude that ethnic heritages seem to endure migration. Apparently, they are also unlikely to be affected by education, generation in the United States, and ethnic self-consciousness. Certain ethnically linked traits (religion, alcohol consumption, political behavior) seem to have remarkable durability despite assimilationist pressures.

This led us to suspect that Old World heritages transported to the New World endure without any conscious intent on the part of "ethnics" because attitudes and behaviors are transmitted early in childhood. Ethnic subcultures, we have hypothesized, are socialization phenomena; that is, they are the result of behavior and attitude patterns transmitted from parent to child without any need for either to realize that these patterns are ethnically linked.

We first examined the utility of this approach in a study of political socialization (1975). Since the model developed from this analysis is the one to be used in our study of alcohol behavior, we will briefly view it here.

POLITICAL SOCIALIZATION

We asked five questions about the political socialization of American ethnics:

1. Are the political values of young people influenced by their ethnic background?
2. If such an influence exists, to what extent is it the result of direct parental socialization, and to what extent does it seem to be a function of an ethnic subculture and operates independently of the young person's propensity to imitate his or her parents' values?
3. If, indeed, there is such a thing as an ethnic political subculture, is it in fact merely a social-class subculture that results in a correlation between ethnicity and social class?
4. Are these differences in family structure among certain American ethnic groups, differences which are predictable from the existing literature?

5. Finally, if such differences in family structure exist, do they correlate with differences in political values?

The issues raised in these questions can be stated in the five-variable model in Figure 2.1. The first variable, ethnic subculture, is a residual variable not specified in the present analysis. It represents those traits, values, experiences, and predispositions that a given ethnic collectivity carries both because of its Old World background and because of its experience since arriving in the United States (the Irish predisposition to political careers, for example). Operational measures for the other four variables—social class, family structure, parent's political value and child's political value—are available in the data we will analyze.

Of the ten paths in the model, path I (ethnicity social class) will be assumed. Social class parents' political values (VI) has already been established by the research of Jennings and his colleagues (Jennings and Niemi 1968; Jennings and Langton 1968). The other eight paths will be examined here. We note that path IX, leading from family structure to the line connecting parent's political value and child's political value, represents an interaction term, that is, the propensity of certain forms of family structure to facilitate or impede direct transmission of a political value from parent to child.

The model hypothesizes four direct paths of political socialization within an ethnic collectivity. Children's political values may be influenced directly by the political value of their parents (X), by the family structure that is peculiar to their ethnic collectivities (VIII), by the social class background of their families (VII), and by those aspects of the ethnic subculture that are not mediated through either family structure or parents' political values (II). We also hypothesize that both family structure and parent's political values are influenced by ethnic subculture and by social class (III, IV, VI).

There is no reason why statistical frequency could not be assigned to each of the paths of our model (whether they come from parametric or nonparametric analysis) save that in the data set we are analyzing there are simply not enough cases in any ethnic group to justify a serious attempt to fit the data to the model. The somewhat complex strategy used here has been imposed upon us by the limited size of each ethnic group in our sample. We think that for those interested in ethnic political socialization to obtain information about a much larger number of respondents within given ethnic groups is of the highest order of importance.

The data we used to answer our questions were taken from the 1965 study directed by M. Kent Jennings (Jennings 1971). In Table 2.1 we present the distribution of families (one parent and one adolescent child) by major ethnic groups. In our analysis we are concerned particularly with four ethnic groups: Irish Catholics, Italian Catholics, Swedish Protestants, and Jews, and comparisons between them and their relationship to a control group of white English American Protestants (See listing of Hypotheses at the end of this Chapter). The theoretical perspectives gained from family-structure literature (to be discussed later) inclined us to expect structural and behavioral differences between these four groups.

ETHNICITY AND THE POLITICAL VALUES OF TWO GENERATIONS

Table 2.2 gives the correlation between parental values and adolescent values for each ethnic group and the rank-order correlations of the groups in the first and second generations. As Jennings and his colleagues (1971) indicated, it is clear that there is only a low to moderate correlation between parental political values and adolescent political values, but it is also clear that the various ethnic groups sort themselves in relatively the same order in both generations. Only one of the rank-order correlations was not significant. Thus, on the ego-strength scale (the scale might be considered to measure "stubbornness") Irish Catholics are second in both generations, but the correlation between parent and adolescent on this variable is only .07. Ego strength seems to be part of the Irish Catholic subculture, but it does not seem to be handed on directly from parent to child. There is, then, some reason to believe on the basis of Table 2.2 that there are ethnic political subcultures which are transmitted to a considerable extent independently of the direct influence of parental values on child values.

Of the four groups we are particularly interested in, Irish Catholic adolescents are substantially above the mean on political efficacy, ego strength, cosmopolitanism, political activity, and political knowledge. They are substantially below the mean on cynicism and on the perception of sharp ideological differences between political parties. In all cases the scores of the Irish Catholic adolescents reflect more or less similar positions on the same scales as their parents, although only on the scale of political cynicism is there a strong correlation between parental and adolescent position. The Irish appear to be political sophisticates in both generations, with a strong sense of political efficacy, high level of cosmopolitanism, a low level of cynicism, and a high level of political activity and knowledge.

Their adolescent Italian co-religionists are beneath the mean on political efficacy, civic tolerance, ego strength, political activity, and political knowledge. In each case they reflect scores beneath the mean of their parents. Italians of both generations seem to be neither political activists nor political sophisticates.

Jews of both generations are beneath the mean on social trust but substantially above it on political efficacy, civic tolerance, cosmopolitanism, political activity, and political knowledge. Indeed, Jews of both generations have the highest rank on the political-knowledge scale and the second-highest rank on the political-activity scale. Jewish teenagers are also second on the cosmopolitanism scale (their parents rank number one) and second on the political-efficacy scale (their parents rank third). Like the Irish, the Jews seem to be both political participators and political sophisticates.

Finally, the Swedish of both generations are above the mean on social trust, civic tolerance, ego strength, cosmopolitanism, political activity, and political knowledge. They are below the mean on the perception of sharp ideological differences between political parties. Swedes, like the Irish and the Jews, are political sophisticates and activists, but they are more likely than Jews and Irish of either generation to be high on social trust and, with the exception of second-generation Jews, high on civic tolerance. Thus, Swedish political culture seems to involve not only political activism and sophistication but also a certain civic-mindedness, which is less likely to be found among the Irish and Jews.

ETHNICITY, PARENTAL VALUES, AND SOCIAL CLASS

There are, apparently, ethnic political subcultures that are passed on from generation to generation with direct parental influence playing only a limited role in the transmission of such political values. But to what extent are these ethnic subcultures in fact social-class status subcultures? To answer this we attempted a multiple-classification analysis in which the dependent variable was the adolescent's political value and the three predictor variables were the political value of the parent (measuring the impact of direct socialization), the education of the head of the family (measuring roughly the family's social status), and the father's religio-ethnic identification. Table 2.3 presents the unadjusted and the standardized *etas* for each of nine dependent variables. The relationship between education and political value is statistically significant seven of the nine times (only social trust and political cynicism seem to be independent of social status as measured by education). The influence of parental values—net of education and ethnicity—is significant eight times, with only adolescent civic tolerance being immune from the influence of the parental value. Finally, ethnicity net of education and parental attitude is statistically related to the adolescent political value eight times, with only the perception of ideological differences between political parties not significantly related to ethnicity.

Ethnicity, then, is a stronger predictor of adolescent values than is the social status of the family (as measured by the head of the family's education) in six of the nine times, and education is a stronger predictor than ethnicity only two of the nine times (civic tolerance and ideology).

Ethnicity is a stronger predictor than parental score on the same value five times, though it is less strong than parental score on the same value four times. It would surely seem that there are ethnic political subcultures that are not the same as class subcultures and that are transmitted across generational lines, in part at least, independent of direct influence of parents on children. The mean adjusted *eta* for ethnicity is 13.7; for education, 12.5; and for parental value, 12.3. All three factors influence adolescent behavior to some extent, and ethnicity is by no means the weakest of the three.

ETHNICITY AND FAMILY STRUCTURE

In a review of the family-structure literature, Strauss argues that much of the research he reviews on family structure indicates that two "reference axes" may be used to array patterns of interaction or personality. Relying on the work of many authors, he contends that the two principal axes in family structure are "power" and "support." He defines *power* as "actions which control, initiate, change, or modify the behavior of another member of the family" (1964:18). *Support* comprises "actions which establish, maintain, or restore, as an end in itself, a positive affective relationship with another family member" (ibid.). A two-by-two model like the one developed by Strauss is presented in Figure 2.2 Strauss suggests that the most effective transmission of parental values will take place in the upper left quadrant, where both power and support are the strongest. He does not suggest, although it seems to follow logically, that the second most effective direct socialization will take place in the upper right quadrant where, while power is low, support is still high. Young people are not forced by power to imitate their parents but are won by the relaxed and democratic styles of the family; they imitate their parents voluntarily. It would also suggest that the least effective direct socialization will occur in the lower left-hand corner, because in a situation where power is strongly concentrated in the family and suport is weak, there will be a propensity to rebel against explicit parental values. Finally, in the lower right, where both support and power are low, socialization will be more effective than it will be in the rebellious lower left quadrant but less effective than in the upper half of the figure. The numbers in the quadrants indicate our expectations of the relative effectiveness of direct socialization.

The literature on ethnic famiy structures in the United States is not extensive, but Italians (about whom the literature is the most extensive) clearly belong in the upper left-hand quadrant (Figure 2.3). The Italian family is warm and affectionate, but power is concentrated in the hands of a strong paternal personage (Tomasi 1972). The Jewish family has traditionally been both strongly affectionate and democratic, if only because of the relative strength of the Jewish mother (Landes and Zborowski 1958; Wolfenstein 1955). Thus, the Jewish family seems to belong in the upper right quadrant. The Irish family is ordinarily described as both unaffectionate and undemocratic, with a very strong father in rural Ireland and an autocratic mother who overwhelms both father and children in urban Ireland and urban United States (Stein 1972; Greeley 1974). The Irish would fit in the lower left-hand quadrant. Finally, the Swedish family, about which much less is known than the other three, seems to belong in the lower right-hand quadrant. The Swedish family is relatively democratic and low in explicit support and affection.

To confirm our hypothesized distribution of the four ethnic family structures and to see whether they can in fact be ranked in the effectiveness of direct political socialization, we looked at a number of questions in the Jennings study (1971) which could measure both the concentration of decision making power and the levels of affection in a family. Since his questions were asked of both generations, it was possible to view family structure from the perspective of both parents and adolescents. An oblique-factor analysis with Kaiser normalization was attempted on a number of these items, and two factors did emerge that seemed to measure roughly support and power. The first factor (power) loads heavily on items measuring the democratic structure of the family (whether decision making is evenly distributed between two parents or whether one parent dominates). The second factor (support) leans heavily on items measuring the children's perceptions of their closeness to their parents and the parents' perceptions of closeness to their parents when they were children.

We would expect the Irish and Italians to be high on the power factor and the Jews and Swedish to be low. We would also anticipate Jews and Italians to be high on the support factor and Irish and Scandinavians low. In Table 2.4 we note that more than half a standard deviation separates the Italians on the support scale and the Italians and the Jews on the power scale. (We should note here, incidentally, that there is no correlation between either the support scale or the power scale and the social status of the family as measured by the education of the head of the family.)

Does family structure, as measured by power and support factors, predict the effectiveness of direct parent-child political socialization? Are the Italians the most effective in transmitting political values to their children and the Irish the least effective? Table 2.5 indicates that the predicated ordering does exist in reality. The average intergenerational correlation on the nine political value scales is .215 for the Italians, .213 for the Jews, .146 for the Scandinavians, and .122 for the Irish Catholics. The Italians and the Jews are virtually tied for first place of the 12 religio-ethnic groups, and the Swedish and the Irish Catholics are at the bottom of the list, with their average intergenerational correlations being higher only than that of the German Protestants. There are not only ethnic political subcultures, there are also ethnic family structures, some of which are much more favorably disposed than others to the direct transmission of political values.

The question arises that, in addition to facilitating or impeding the effectiveness of the family as a direct agent of political socialization, might it be that the structure of the family itself may be involved in the transmission of political values? For example, are Italian adolescents less likely to be politically involved not only because their parents are less likely to be involved but also because there is something in the dynamic of Italian family life which leads, of itself and independent of parental values, to lower levels of political interest or concern? Here we have come full circle in our argument. While there is little evidence in general American society (as noted by Jennings and his colleagues) that family structure influences political values, perhaps within certain ethnic groups family structure influences political values. We are clearly within a very speculative area, and we are using measures designed for purposes other than those for which we use them here. Hence, this phase of our analysis must be considered extremely tentative.

First of all, there is in the general population only one correlation between the two family structures scales and the nine political value scales we are using that is higher than .1, and that is a correlation of .12 between the power factor and the perception of sharp ideological differences between political parties. Thus, although our measures are different from Jennings', we come to the same conclusion that for the national population family structure does not seem to influence the political values of adolescents.

But does family structure exercise such influence within the various ethnic subcollectivities? The Italian family is the best test case, because Italian political participation is low and the Italian family is strong on power and support, which might be thought to lend the family a self-sufficiency that would obviate the need for adolescents to involve themselves in other institutions.

Table 2.5 generally confirms this expectation. The stronger family support is in the Italian family, the weaker is trust, tolerance, cosmopolitanism, and political knowledge. Tolerance and political knowledge also correlate negatively with power in the Italian family, although political activity correlates positively with power. Its strong support mechanisms, then, incline the offspring of Italian families to be less concerned about the outside world (low on both cosmopolitanism and political knowledge) and also more suspicious of the outside world (low on trust and tolerance). Furthermore, the strong concentration of power in the Italian family also correlates negatively with interest and positively with suspicion—though it is in those Italian families where power is most strongly concentrated that somewhat higher levels of political activity are likely to be found.

For the Jewish family one might expect just the opposite. Political participation and the absence of suspicion might be heightened by the democratic style of the family and perhaps reinforced by its strong internal cohesion and warmth. It indeed turns out to be the case that the more democratic the Jewish family is (that is, the lower on the power scale), the more tolerant adolescents are and the more likely they are to be involved in political activity. Furthermore, ego strength (stubborness), on which Jewish adolescents are much more likely to score higher than their parents (see Table 2.6), also correlates negatively with power (and hence positively with democratic style). The more democratic the family the stronger the ego strength of the Jewish adolescent. Power in the Jewish family correlates positively only with cosmopolitanism and there are no correlations between political values and family support for the Jewish family.

It is somewhat harder to elaborate expectations for the Irish family. But one might predict that interest in politics for the Irish could result from strong family power constraints. Irish youngsters are so busy calculating the implicit, unspoken conflicts over power in their families that they have a predisposition to be interested in the exercise of power wherever it occurs. However, it would only be in the Irish families where there is some encouragement and warmth that children could work up enough courage to be actually involved in politics.

It is precisely in the high-power-concentration Irish families where one is most likely to find higher scores of political knowledge—and also more cynicism, weakened ego strength, and weaker social trust. Furthermore, while the support level is low in the Irish family, still it is in those families where there is more support than the average that the higher level of political activity is to be found, as well as a lower propensity to see sharp ideological cleavage between the parties.

Finally, one might ask whether the stronger "civic-mindedness" of Swedish adolescents might relate to the democratic structure of the Swedish family. In fact, however, the opposite seems to be the case. Civic trust (and political knowledge) relate negatively not to power but to support in the Swedish family. One finds higher levels of trust and of political knowledge precisely in those Swedish families where affection seems to be the lowest. In three of the four cases, then, our tentative expectations about the relationship between family structure and political values were at least partially confirmed. Only with Swedes could we find no support for our expectations.

It is interesting to note in Table 2.6 the different relationships that family structures have for various ethnic groups on political knowledge and political activity. For Italians political activity correlates positively with a strong concentration of power in the family; for Jews it correlates negatively. For the Irish there is a positive correlation between political activity and the support factor. Political knowledge correlated positively with power concentration for the Irish and negatively with power concentration for Italians. It correlates negatively with support for both Swedes and Italians. The Irish who are the most likely to be politically knowledgable come from power-concentrated families. The Swedish who are the most likely to be politically knowledgable come from low-support families. Italians with high political knowledge come from families with weak power concentrations and weak social support. The activist Italians come from high-power families, activist Jews from low-power families, and activist Irish from high-support families. We conclude, then, that while the fit is not perfect and many uncertainties and obscurities remain, there is a relationship between family structure and political values in various ethnic collectivities. These relationships run one way in some ethnic groups and in the opposite direction in others.

There are ethnic subcultures that transmit different political values to the children born within these cultures. Ethnic subcultures have different family structures; these family structures affect the strength of the direct parent-child political socialization, with the family structures in some ethnic subcultures being much more successful at passing the explicit values of parents on to the children. But in addition the family structure itself, quite independently of the specific values of the parents, is also a socializing institution that transmits the ethnic cultures independently of explicit parental values. Italians, for example, are likely to be low political participators because their parents are low political participators, because the strength and warmth of the Italian family more effectively communicates low participation values across generational lines, and because the structure itself—independent of specific parental attitudes—produces lower levels of political interest and higher levels of political suspicion.

Jews are high political participators in part because of higher social status, in part because Jewish parents are more likely to be high participators, in part because Jewish family structure facilitates the direct transmission of parents' participation values to their children, and finally because the democratic structure of the family itself, independent of specific parental values, creates a higher propensity for political activism.

Ethnic political cultures, then, are handed on, in part, directly through children's imitation of their parents and, in part, both directly and indirectly because family structure acts as an independent variable with an impact of its own for some ethnic groups on some political values.

What happens to our socialization model when various controls are introduced for selected political values on which differences between two groups are considerable? Tables 2.7 and 2.8 illustrate two examples.

Jewish adolescents and Italian adolescents are rather different from each other both in their scores on political activity and civic tolerance, with

Jews in both cases having the higher scores. The difference in political activity is diminished by 17 points by a control for parental education. None of the factors in the model seem to have much impact. When parental education is taken into account, Jewish adolescents are still more likely to be politically active than Italian adolescents, though the difference has been narrowed somewhat.

On the subject of civic tolerance, however, the model operates in another manner. Jewish adolescents are 21 points higher on civic tolerance than Italians. When parental values are taken into account, the difference diminishes to 16. When education is added to the model, the differences in civic tolerance between Italians and Jews diminish altogether. Hence, adolescent Jews are higher on civic tolerance than Italians because their parents are higher on civic tolerance and because their parents are better educated.

Then there are some variables on which the model has almost no impact. The Irish are somewhat more likely than the Jews to score high on social trust (Table 2.8), but none of the controls introduced affect the difference very much. The slight propensity of Irish adolescents to be more trusting than Jews is not a function of education or parental values or family structure, and to the extent that it represents a meanful difference at all it must be attributed to some residual cultural difference not accounted for by our model.

SOCIALIZATION TO ALCOHOL

We propose to use the same basic approach to study alcohol subcultures as we used in our study of political subcultures. Both the personality and the cultural aproaches to ethnic differences in drinking assume, implicitly at least, the family as a unit of cultural transmission. Drinking patterns are indisputably the result of the socialization process, and socialization takes place primarily, though not exclusively, in the family context. It was our intention in our research to study drinking patterns as learned behavior which is acquired to a considerable extent in the family context. It is not inconceivable that the basic reason that members of one ethnic group drink more than those of other groups is that their parents drank more. One need not appeal either to the family structure or the general culture of an ethnic group until one has exluded the possibility that drinking behavior is largely learned directly from one's parents merely by imitation. The Irish may drink more because their parents drank more, and their parents may have drunk more because *their* parents drank more. Social and cultural phenomena of the past (the Famine and immigration) may have set in motion patterns of behavior which get passed on from generation to generation with family structure and cultural norms having little relationship to such transmission.

The application of the political socialization model to alcohol socialization results in Figure 2.3. Variable 1 is the attitude of members of all three generations about drinking behavior independent of actual behavior of parents. (To obtain third-generation data we asked retrospective questions of our adult respondents about their parents' friends, as well as asking for the information about the parents' generation. Variables 2, 3, and 8 represent the drinking behavior of father, mother, and child (as tapped by a number of different measurements). The strength of the direct path between father's drinking behavior and that of the adolescent (2 and 8) and between mother's and adolescent's drinking behavior (3 and 8) indicate how much "socialization-as-imitation" is occurring within a given group. The relative size of the former to the latter will indicate whether the father's or the mother's behavior is the more influential, or whether same-sex or cross-sex influence is occurring. Variable 4 stands for the quality of the relationship between the parents. It will enable us to determine whether stress in the parental relationship leads to a higher level of adolescent alcohol use, and whether this differs between ethnic groups. Variables 5 and 6 represent the two dimensions of family structure—power and support. Variable 7 stands for such questions as the age at the time of the first drink, drinking in the family context, and the use of drink in ritual celebrations and ceremonies.*

This model can be applied to each of the ethnic groups studied and should enable us to partial out the relative influences in ethnic alcohol socialization of culture, imitation and family structure.

HYPOTHESES

From the existing literature on ethnicity and alcohol use and ethnicity and socialization we derived the following guiding hypotheses to be tested against the data:

1. In both parental and adolescent generations, the five ethnic groups being studied, including the English as our control group, would show the following pattern:

    a. Frequency of nonabstainers: Irish, Jewish, Italian, Swedish, English.
    b. Frequency of drinking: Irish, English, Swedish, Italian, Jewish.
    c. Among those who drink, the number of drinks at a sitting: Irish, English, Swedish, Italian, Jewish.

*Within variables 5 and 6 one might also include the personality characteristics that are presumed to flow from various constellations of power and support in the family structure. The dotted lines between 2 and 4 and 3 and 4 represent the very real possibility that drinking behavior will affect the quality of parents' relationships.

d. Among those who drink, the frequency of serious drink problems: English, Irish, Swedish, Jewish, Italian.
   e. Among those who drink, the frequency of major trouble with drinking: English, Irish, Swedish, Italian, Jewish.

2. There will be a high level of direct imitation of parental behavior among adolescents. We hypothesized, therefore, that socialization to alcohol is more like religious socialization than political socialization and that the direct-path coefficient between parental behavior and adolescent behavior will be rather high.

3. Along with Ullman (1958), we hypothesized that the greater the diversity of attitudes and values (measured by the standard deviation) on drinking within a given group, the more likely that group is to experience serious alcohol problems and potential alcoholism.

4. In those groups, such as Italians and Jews, in which there is the greatest consistency of cultural norms in the three generations, there will be the least likelihood of serious drink problems or potential alcoholism.

5. We expected family structure (as measured by the POWER dimension, the SUPPORT dimension, and the quality of relationship between husband and wife) to make a direct contribution (through personality) to their children's drinking behavior only when there is a high level of tolerance for drinking in the ethnic community and when the typical family structure of an ethnic community predisposes some of its adolescent children to the kinds of personality weakness for which excessive drinking might be an escape.

In other words, one could legitimately expect high POWER and low SUPPORT to correlate with serious drinking problems for the Irish. A young person coming from a rigid, unaffectionate Irish family will be more likely to exhibit alcoholic propensities than a young person coming from a Jewish family with exactly the same rigidity and lack of affection.

6. We also hypothesized tentatively that family structure will have a direct influence on drinking behavior and particularly on serious drinking problems when there is a high level of drinking in the group, a strong parental-adolescent direct correlation, and a family structure which might lead to personality problems for which excessive drinking could be an escape. (Such might be the case for Swedes and English.)

The methodology of the project is discussed in appendices to this volume. Because of the limitations of financial resources, we chose four cities in which the ethnic groups we were studying were most likely to be concentrated. Respondent families were chosen by random-digit telephone calls. Self-administered questionnaires were used because there is evidence that honest answers are more likely to be obtained on the subject of alcohol with this type of procedure. One parent and one adolescent in each family (randomly chosen for sex) filled out the questionnaire; 90 percent of those who were screened into the sample accepted questionnaires, and 80 percent of those who accepted questionnaires returned them. It should be noted that the group mean score from which variations are measured in subsequent chapters is an "artificial" mean; that is to say, it is the mean score of the ethnic groups that constitute the sample and not the mean score of the total U.S. population or of the total population in the four cities. It is, rather, the average score only of the population from the cities where the selected ethnic groups live.

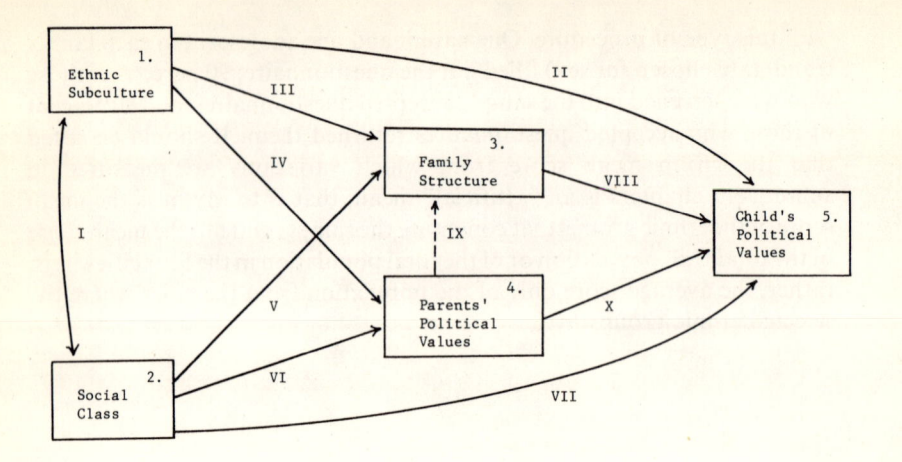

Fig. 2.1 A Model for Political Socialization Within an Ethnic Collectivity.

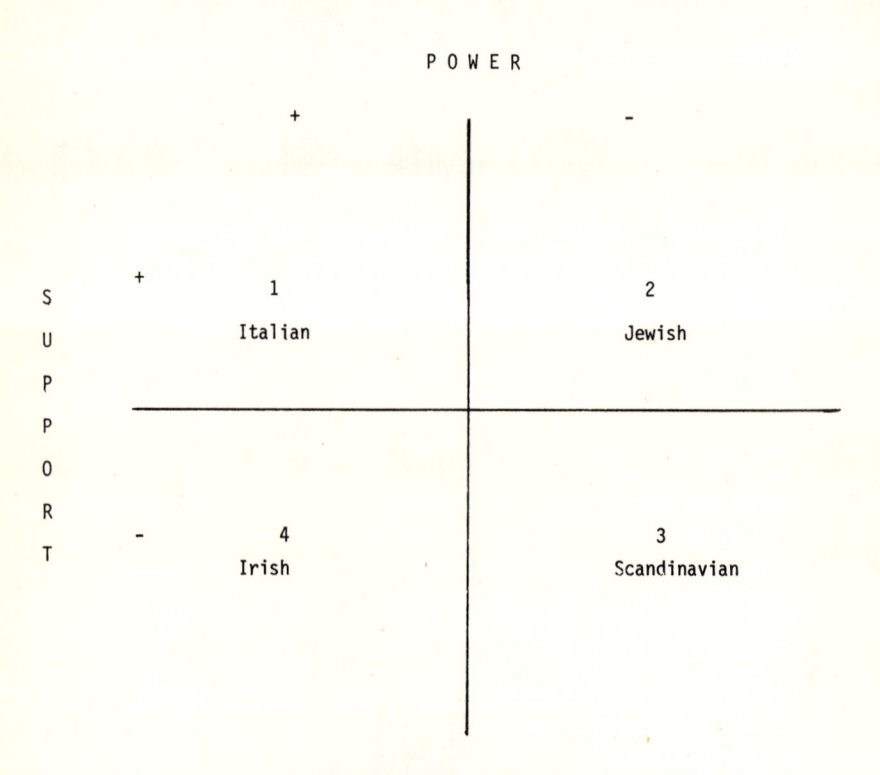

Fig. 2.2 Power, Support, and a Hypothesized Ranking of Value Transmission Effectiveness with the Hypothesized Distribution of Four Ethnic Groups.

30   *Ethnic Drinking Subcultures*

TABLE 2.1

DISTRIBUTION OF AMERICAN RELIGIO-ETHNIC GROUPS IN
JENNINGS' INTERGENERATIONAL SURVEY

ETHNIC GROUP	Number
White	
Protestant	
British	268
Irish	77
Scandinavian	65
German	200
Other	502
Catholic	
Irish	49
German	57
East European	45
Italian	62
Spanish-Speaking	25
Jewish	76
Black	183

TABLE 2.2

POLITICAL VALUES AMONG FOUR AMERICAN ETHNIC GROUPS BY GENERATION

Political Value	Irish Parents Score[a]	Irish Parents Rank[b]	Irish Children Score[a]	Irish Children Rank[b]	r*	Italians Parents Score[a]	Italians Parents Rank[b]	Italians Children Score[a]	Italians Children Rank[b]	r*
Social Trust	24	3	07	6	.05	-16	9	02	9	.27
Civil Tolerance	24	3	07	6	.17	-26	12	-02	8	.28
Political Efficacy	13	5	33	3	.08	-08	8	-04	7	.04
Ego Strength	21	2	26	2	.07	-22	10	-43	12	.03
Cosmopolitanism	27	3	25	3	-.03	21	4	-01	9	.28
Political Cynicism	-40	12	-10	7	.39	-38	11	-18	10	.22
Political Activity	14	5	28	1	.15	-06	9	-11	11	.24
Political Knowledge	51	2	28	2	.14	08	7	-17	10	.39
Ideology	-30	10	-12	10	-.02	24	3	01	4	.36

Political Value	Scandinavians Parents Score[a]	Scandinavians Parents Rank[b]	Scandinavians Children Score[a]	Scandinavians Children Rank[b]	r*	Jews Parents Score[a]	Jews Parents Rank[b]	Jews Children Score[a]	Jews Children Rank[b]	r*
Social Trust	39	1	18	3	.02	-12	7	-08	10	.24
Civic Tolerance	43	1	10	5	.28	35	2	16	4	.15
Political Efficacy	35	1	10	5	.01	24	3	35	2	.21
Ego Strength	09	4	43	1	.09	-36	11	11	4	.12
Cosmopolitanism	14	6	41	1	.37	35	1	35	2	.11
Political Cynicism	08	4	-16	8	.22	11	3	-06	6	.04
Political Activity	50	1	10	4	.04	39	2	25	2	.24
Political Knowledge	26	4	19	4	.12	63	1	65	1	.37
Ideology	-31	11	-12	10	.27	-47	12	-11	9	.45

[a] Scores represent standardized points deviating from mean for generation. 1.00 = 1 standard deviation. Scores are the percentage of standard deviation above or below the mean.

[b] Rank is the rank of the group within its own generation among the twelve major groups.

*Correlation between parental score and adolescent score in each ethnic group.

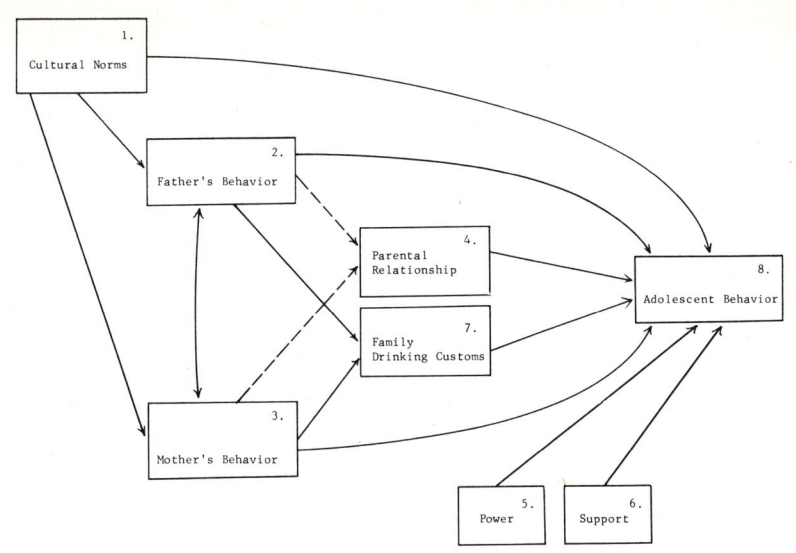

Fig. 2.3 General Model of Alcohol Socialization.

TABLE 2.3

ADOLESCENT POLITICAL VALUES BY EDUCATION OF PARENT, PARENTAL ETHNICITY AND PARENTAL POLITICAL VALUE: A MULTIPLE CLASSIFICATION ANALYSIS

Political Value	Unadjusted Era			Adjusted Era		
	Education	Parental Value	Ethnicity	Education	Parental Value	Ethnicity
Social trust	.07	.12	.21	.04	.08	.19
Civic tolerance	.28	.13	.19	.25	.06	.12
Political efficacy	.18	.14	.18	.13	.08	.15
Ego strength	.13	.14	.19	.09	.12	.17
Cosmopolitanism	.15	.21	.16	.10	.19	.12
Political cynicism	.02	.16	.12	.02	.16	.12
Political activity	.14	.11	.13	.13	.08	.13
Political knowledge	.29	.33	.18	.16	.21	.18
Ideology	.23	.20	.11	.19	.14	.08

TABLE 2.4

RANK ORDER OF FOUR AMERICAN ETHNIC GROUPS ON THE
SUPPORT AND POWER SCALES
(Standardized Points)

Support		Power	
Ethnic Group	Score	Ethnic Group	Score
Italian Catholics	33	Italian Catholics	19
Jews	14	Irish Catholics	08
Irish Catholics	-19	Scandinavian Protesttants	-09
Scandinavian Protestants	-24	Jews	-32

TABLE 2.5

RANK ORDER OF AMERICAN ETHNIC GROUPS ON AVERAGE CORRELATION OF NINE
POLITICAL VALUE SCALES BETWEEN PARENTS AND ADOLESCENTS

Ethnic Group	Score
<u>Italian Catholic</u>	.215
<u>Jewish</u>	.213
East European Catholic	.183
Irish Protestant	.172
German Catholic	.163
Spanish speaking	.163
American Protestant	.160
Black	.152
British	.151
<u>Scandinavian</u>	.146
<u>Irish Catholic</u>	.122
German Protestant	.105

34   Ethnic Drinking Subcultures

TABLE 2.6

CORRELATIONS BETWEEN FAMILY STRUCTURES AND POLITICAL VALUES*

Political Value	Scandinavian Support	Scandinavian Power	Irish Support	Irish Power	Italian Support	Italian Power	Jewish Support	Jewish Power
Social Trust	-.16	--	--	-.37	-.27	--	--	--
Tolerance	--	--	--	--	-.45	-.15	--	-.25
Efficacy	--	--	--	--	--	--	--	--
Ego strength	--	--	--	-.29	--	--	--	-.18
Cosmopolitanism	--	--	--	--	-.31	--	--	.26
Political cynicism	--	--	--	.24	-.21	--	--	--
Political activity	--	--	.20	--	--	.21	--	.20
Political knowledge	-.19	--	-.33	.16	-.18	-.27	--	--
Ideology	--	--	--	--	--	-.23	--	--

*Only correlations larger than .15 are shown.

TABLE 2.7

DIFFERENCES BETWEEN ITALIAN AND JEWISH ADOLESCENTS
IN TWO POLITICAL VALUES

(Jewish "Lead" in Standardized Points)*

	Political Activity	Civic Tolerance
Raw differences	43	21
Net of parental value	41	16
Net of parental value and parental education	24	00
Net of parental value, education and power factor	23	00
Net of parental value, education, power factor and support factor	24	00

* Scores were obtained by multiple-classification analysis with two categories (above and below the mean) for the value and factor scores and three categories for education (grammar, high school, and college).

Approaches to Ethnicity

TABLE 2.8

DIFFERENCES BETWEEN IRISH AND JEWISH ADOLESCENTS IN SOCIAL TRUST
(Irish "lead" in standardized points)

Raw differences	13
Net of parental value	10
Net of parental value and parental education	11
Net of parental value, education, and power factor	12
Net of parental value, education, power factor and support factor	11

CHAPTER THREE
Drinking Subcultures

Before turning to a description of drinking subcultures, it is appropriate to ask whether the family-structure variables devised for the study of political socialization were replicated in the data collected in the present project. The scores were not the same, of course, because in the political socialization study the measure was a deviation from the national mean; in the present project the measure was deviation from the mean composed of the "artificial" population of the five ethnic groups investigated. Table 3.1A shows, however, that the ordering of the groups is roughly the same in both samples on POWER and SUPPORT in existing families. The Irish and Italians are high on POWER, while Swedes and Jews are low. Italians and Jews are higher on SUPPORT than are Irish and Swedes. Thus, the same two-by-two paradigm on POWER and SUPPORT that we had anticipated in the political study is replicated in the alcohol study.

When one turns to the description by our adult respondents of their families of origin, two notable differences appear. Even though their families are very democratic, Jewish adult respondents remember authoritarian families of origin, and, instead of being on the bottom of the POWER score in parental generation, they are on the top. Similarly, even though their own family life is very affectionate, Italian adult respondents recollect very low levels of SUPPORT in their families of origin. It would appear, then, that either there are selective recollections of the structure of family life at the grandparental generation or there have been notable shifts in the structure of Italians and Jewish family life between the grandparental and the parental generations. Such a shift offers the possibility for extremely interesting research on the history of the American family (Table 3.1B).

It is also useful at the beginning of this description to determine how the ethnic groups in both generations score on "efficacy" scales, which are designed to measure psychological "self-confidence." One would expect from previous literature on drinking that Jews would tend to score high on such scales and the Irish would score low (Table 3.1C). In both generations the Jewish score is higher than the Irish score—20 standardized points in the parental generation and 13 standardized points in the adolescent generation. (The scales are composed of different items in the respective generations, since several of the adult questions were not appropriate for adolescents.) In addition in both generations the two Catholic groups are lower on the scale than the three non-Catholic groups. We shall defer to subsequent chapters the question of what impact this psychological self-confidence has on drinking behavior. (For a discussion of Catholic family structure, see Greeley and McCready, 1978.)

On the basis of the hypotheses advanced in Chapter 2, we would expect that the groups would rank themselves in terms of alcohol consumption in the following order: Irish, Swedes, Italians, Jews. The Irish and Swedes will be more likely to have alcohol problems than will Italians and Jews, the Irish more likely than Swedes, Jews less likely than Italians. The Irish and Swedes will be in relatively high drinking environments, the Italians and Jews in relatively low drinking environments. In our survey we have retrospective information about grandparental generation, interview data with both parents and adolescent children. Thus, our expectations about alcohol subcultures may be tested in all three generations.

In the grandparental generation the level of alcohol consumption roughly follows our expectations. Fathers and mothers of the Irish respondents were the most likely to drink heavily, while Jews were the least likely to drink heavily (Table 3.2). Italian grandparents, however, were somewhat more likely to drink than Swedish grandparents, and indeed there was little difference between Italian and Irish grandparents in the proportion of fathers drinking daily or more often and mothers drinking almost daily or more often. The Italians were the most likely (35 percent) to say their parents always served drinks to guests, followed by the Irish (20 percent), the Swedes (9 percent), and the Jews (6 percent). Thus, we are forced, on the basis of our retrospective information about the grandparental generation, to modify somewhat our expectations about the Italian drinking subculture. On the basis of the performances of the grandparents, we would expect that if the Italian drinking subculture perdures, in terms of the quantity of drinking, Italians would be ahead of the Swedes and distinguishable from the Irish only at the top end of the drinking levels, that is, men who drink twice a day or more (19 percent of the Irish and 13 percent of the Italian grandfathers).

But if they drink as much as the Irish, the Italians are substantially less likely to have drinking problems. Forty percent of our Irish respondents reported a drinking problem in the home, as opposed to 13 percent of the Italian respondents (and 30 percent of the Swedish respondents and 4 percent of the Jewish respondents). In each of the ethnic groups, about 75 percent of the drinking problems in the home were problems with the father; others were equally distributed among grandparents, uncles or aunts, older brothers, and mothers.

With the slight modification of Italians being somewhat heavier drinkers in the grandparental generation than the previous literature would have led us to expect, we find sharply differentiated ethnic drinking subcultures existing in the generation of the grandparents. The Irish are heavy drinkers with serious problems, Italians are heavy drinkers with a minimum of serious problems, Swedes drink less than the Italians but are more likely to have drinking problems, and Jews are low on all measures.

The English Protestant group is more likely to drink than Jews but generally less likely to drink than the other three ethnic groups. About 20 percent of the English Protestant families—more than Jews and Italians and less than the Irish and Swedes—report a drinking problem in their homes when they were growing up.

The pattern laid out in the grandparental generation is duplicated in the parental generation (Table 3.2). While virtually all our respondents have drunk at one time, the Irish and the Swedes are, in fact, somewhat less likely to be drinking now than the Italians and the Jews and English (meaning a higher proportion of the Irish and the Swedes have stopped drinking); the Irish are still the most likely to say they drink almost every day or more (48 percent of the men, 13 percent of the women). Italians are in second place (40 percent of the men and 11 percent of the women), Swedes are in third place (31 and 9 percent), and Jews are fourth with 10 percent of the men and 5 percent of the women drinking almost every day.

The same order exists in the proportion having a predinner drink every day (with the Swedes and the Italians virtually tied for second place) in the proportion describing themselves as "heavy drinkers" and the proportion saying they would miss drinking a lot (though in this last item, the Swedes are ahead of the Italians). On all of these indicators, except the proportion that would miss drinking a lot, the English Protestant comparative group is more like the Irish Catholic heavy-drinking group than it is like any of the other ethnic groups. It is interesting that a very notable change in drinking behavior has occurred among English Protestants between the grandparental and parental generations. Perhaps this is the result of the movement from rural into urban areas. As we shall see subsequently, a similar change has occurred in the adolescent generation, so that English Protestants, once a relatively moderate drinking group seem to drink almost as much as the Irish in the parental generation and in the adolescent generation they drink even more.

There are distinctive patterns in the kind of alcohol consumed. The Irish (and the English) are the most likely to consume beer, the Italians, as one might expect, by far the most likely to consume wine; Jews occupy second place, with a little less than 20 percent saying they drink wine two or three times a week. All three of the Gentile ethnic groups (Irish, Italians, and Swedes) indicate that about 20 percent of the men and a little less than 10 percent of the women drink hard liquor three or four times a week. The relatively high level frequency of wine consumption among Italians and Jews would be expected on the basis of the literature, since wine is ceremonial for the Jews and food for the Italians.

Irish men drink the most beer at a time—2.5 bottles or cans at a sitting—followed by Italians (2.2), English (2.0), Swedes (1.8). and Jews (less than one full bottle when they drink beer). Italian and Jewish men are also not only the most likely to drink wine frequently; they also drink the most (2.3 and 2.5 glasses respectively), and there is little difference among the men in all the Gentile groups in the mean number of drinks of hard liquor consumed on a single occasion (two drinks or slightly more). Thus, the Irish and Swedes are more likely to turn to beer for their alcohol, the Italians and Jews are more likely to turn to wine, the Jews are less likely to drink hard liquor than Gentiles, and, save for wine, they drink less than Gentiles of each of the three varieties of alcohol (Table 3.3).

A scale was constructed to estimate the total annual amount of ethanol consumption for each respondent based on the estimate of the quantity of ethanol in each can of beer, glass of wine or drink or hard liquor (Table 3.4). There were virtually no differences between the two Catholic ethnic groups and the sheer amount of alcohol consumed each year. Irish men consumed 380 ounces and Italian men 389 ounces; Irish women accounted for 124 ounces, Italian women 133 ounces. English men were in third place (350 ounces), while English women consumed more ethanol than the women in any of the other ethnic groups (144 ounces). Swedish women were in second place in their ethanol consumption (139) ounces, so that Protestant women, on the average, drink slightly more ethanol than do Catholic women. Jewish drinking remains the smallest of all, with men consuming 148 ounces of ethanol (only slightly more than the women in the other four groups) and Jewish women drinking only 90 ounces of ethanol a year.

The Irish and Swedes, however, are more likely to have higher-levels of ethanol intake from hard liquor than do the Italians among both men and women, so that the similarity in total ethanol consumption between the Italians and the Irish is accounted for by Italian wine consumption. English Protestant women annually drink over 100 ounces of ethanol in hard liquor, as opposed to 79 ounces for the Irish, 76 ounces for Swedes, 67 ounces for Italians, and a mere 49 ounces for Jews.

In terms of alcohol consumption, then, there is a basic intergenerational similarity, with Italians, Irish, and Swedes drinking heavily, and Jews drinking relatively little, while the English men and women have moved from a moderate middle ground between the immigrants and the Jews to being heavy drinkers and, in the case of English women, the heaviest drinkers of all.

We hypothesized for both sexes that there would be differences according to ethnic background not merely in the level of drinking but in the drinking environment in which members of the various ethnic groups moved. In Table 3.5 we can observe that this expectation is sustained. The Irish, followed by Italians, Swedes and Jews, in that order, are most likely to say that drinks are served nearly every time that friends get together and that more than half of their friends drink "a lot." The two Catholic groups are also more likely than the three non-Catholic groups to say that they usually serve drinks to guests when they visit. When the responses to these three questions are put together into a single "drinking environment" scale, it becomes evident that there are striking differences in the drinking environments of each ethnic group. The Irish men are 30 standardized points above the mean, while Jewish men are 43 standardized points below—a total difference of more then three-quarters of a standard deviation for the drinking environments of these two extremes of alcohol subcultures. Italians are slightly below the mean (9 points), while Swedish and English men are slightly above it (4 and 17 points, respectively).

The differences are less sharp in the drinking environments of women. Irish women are more likely than Italian, Jewish and Swedish women to report a high drinking environment. English women, as we have seen, consume more ethanol a year than any other group of women, and are also more likely (more than one-third of a standard deviation more likely than the Jews) to describe a relatively heavy drinking environment.

The strongest confirmation of our expectations about drinking subcultures, however, is to found in the area of drinking problems. Using the time-honored six-item drinking-problem scale (Table 3.6), we observe that on virtually all measures, Irish men and Irish women are by far the most likely to describe themselves as engaging in "problem" drinking behavior, with the Swedes and Italians in an intermediate position, and Jews extremely low in their problem drinking.

When the six problem-drinking items are combined into a single drinking-problem scale, Irish are half a standard deviation above the mean in drinking problems, Jewish men a quarter of a standard deviation below the mean, Swedish men are 30 standardized points above the mean, and Italian men 14 standardized points above the mean—all in the precise order predicted by our hypotheses. English men have the second highest scores on the problem-drinking scale; but curiously enough, despite their high drinking level, English women have a score on the scale almost as low as Jewish women (–28 points and –34 points). There is little difference between Irish women and Swedish women in their score on the problem-drinking scale (–14 for the Irish and –15 for the Swedes). However, Italian women have a higher score (–5 points) on the problem-drinking scale than do Irish women.

Thus, with the single exception of the relatively high score of Italian women on the problem-drinking scale, the two sexes and the four ethnic groups sort themselves out in the precise order that previous literature and our hypotheses would have led us to expect. With some minor exceptions, dealing mostly with the drinking behavior of English Protestants and an occasional change in relative position of the Italians and Swedes, the second-generation drinking subculture is remarkably similar to that of the first generation in so far as Irish, Italians, and Swedes are heavy drinkers, Jews are light drinkers, and the Irish are the most likely to be in heavy drinking environments, followed by Swedes, Italians, and Jews. Drinking subculture has persisted from the grandparental to the parental generation. The next question concerns whether it perdures into the adolescent generation.

Before we address ourselves to that question, however, two observations must be made. First of all, both problem drinking and drinking-environment questions that are pertinent to an adult generation are not pertinent to a teenage generation. Hence, different items must be used in both the problem-drinking and drinking-environment scales. There is therefore no reason to expect that standardized scores on these scales will be comparable with those on the adult scales. To confirm the durability of the drinking subculture, it is necessary merely that the groups score on the adolescent scale in the same relative order that they do on the respective adult scales.

Second, during adolescence patterns of drinking behavior are only beginning to emerge. One cannot expect subcultural differences to be as sharply pronounced among adolescents as they are among adults. This is because it is reasonable to assume that young people have yet to acquire permanent orientations toward drinking and because the influence of the peer group is likely to be much more powerful in adolescence than it is in adulthood (an expectation which we will find strongly confirmed in a subsequent chapter).

Adolescents drink much less than their parents (though they seem to be starting earlier and catching up rapidly). Hence, we are less likely to find differences among them in levels of alcohol consumption of the sort that we find among their parents. Italian and Jewish adolescents are more likely to drink than the Swedish, Irish, and English teenagers (Table 3.7). Among the men, Italians and Jews start at a slightly earlier age than the Irish. The average age at which our drinking teenagers began to drink is between 7 and 9 years lower than the age reported for their parents in Table 3.3, but since approximately one-third of the teenagers do not drink yet the average age is likely to go up somewhat if these questions are asked again when our sample of adolescents are in their middle twenties. Nonetheless, it seems reasonable to say that today's adolescents will begin to drink about five years earlier than their parents, though there is some possibility that parents may advance somewhat their recollection of the age at which they began to drink.

Irish young men (though not Irish young women) are more likely than members of the other three ethnic groups to say that they drink two or three times a month or more and that they are high once a month or more (Table 3.8). English young men, however, are the most likely of all to report drinking several times a month and being high once a month, and English young women are also the most likely to say that they drink two or three times a month or more. Jews are the least likely to say they are high once a month or more, with Italian and Swedish males intermediate between Irish and Jews in this respect.

Wine drinking, as one might expect from parental behavior, is more frequent among Italians and Jews than it is among other groups, though the Irish "advantage" in the consumption of beer over the Italians is not replicated in the adolescent generation. In fact, the total ethanol consumption of Irish adolescent men (56 ounces) is lower than that of Italians (82 ounces), English (85 ounces), and Jews (62 ounces); and Irish young women (44 ounces) trail Italians (53 ounces) and English (49 ounces), though Jewish young women consume substantially less alcohol (28 ounces) than Irish young women. (Table 3.9.) Irish young women, however, are the most likely of all the adolescents to consume hard liquor (22 ounces); indeed, they drink more hard liquor than do their male counterparts; but only among the Swedish adolescents is there more hard liquor consumption for men than women. (Perhaps this is because it is easier for boys to purchase beer, while with proper clothes and makeup, girls can more easily be served in a cocktail lounge.)

Thus, it would not appear that, as far as the amount of liquor consumed is concerned the pattern of high Irish and low Jewish drinking is generally sustained in the adolescent generation. But at least some specifics of the adult drinking subculture do perdure. Italians and Jews are the most likely to drink wine, and if the very heavy drinking English teenagers are excluded, Irish young men are the most likely to drink two or three times a month and the most likely to be high once a month or more.

However, when one turns to drinking environments (Table 3.10), the adolescent pattern is quite similar to the adult pattern. The differences are not as great as drinking-environment differences recorded in Table 3.5, but the questions are entirely different; thus, the pertinent issue is whether the groups arrange themselves in roughly the same order. Irish young men and women are in the heaviest drinking environments and Jews, both men and women, are in the lightest drinking environments, with Italians and Swedes between them, the Italians somewhat more likely to be in heavy drinking environments than the Swedes. (This is a different ordering from Table 3.5 as far as young men are concerned. Swedish adult males are somewhat more likely than Italian adult males to be in a heavy drinking environment.)

It is in the matter of drinking problems, however, that we encounter the most precise duplication among adolescents of the parental drinking subculture (Table 3.11). In the adolescent generation boys score on drinking problems almost exactly as the men, with Irish men high on the scale, Jewish men low, English, Swedish, and Italian young men in the middle. Similarly, Italian young women, like Italian adult women, have the highest score on the drinking-problem scale; and Jews have the lowest score. The highest drinking-problem score of all among adolescents, however, is to be found among the English males (38 standardized points); Irish young women (-5 points) are second only to Jews (-38 points) in low scores on the drinking-problem scale—though it is a distant second

The existence of separate drinking subcultures among adolescents is *not* confirmed by the sheer amounts of liquor consumed by young people. The Irish, however, still drink most often, are the most likely to drink two or three times a month or more, are the most likely to get high once a month or more, and have the highest scores on the drinking-environment scale. Moreover, Irish men also have the highest score (second to the English) on the drinking problem scale. Jews, on the other hand, are the least likely to get high once a month and have the lowest scores on both the drinking environment and drinking-problem scales. Jews and Italians are the most likely to drink wine, and in both the adolescent and adult generations Italian women are the most likely to report drinking problems. All things considered, then, the drinking subcultures show remarkable durability even in the adolescent generation, and while it remains to be seen whether, as they grow into maturity, their drinking consumption levels will fall into patterns not unlike those exhibited by their parents, it would seem that even in adolescence the two extreme drinking subcultures, Irish and Jewish, have already sharply differentiated themselves in drunkenness, drinking environment, and drinking problems; and this despite the fact that it is necessary to use entirely different items to measure both environment and problem in the adolescent generation.

In all three generations, then, there are sharply differentiated drinking subcultures with remarkable continuity for all groups but the English where heavy drinking seems to be increasing with each generation. The Irish are most likely to be problem drinkers in all three generations, the Jews are least likely to be problem drinkers, and the Italians and the Swedes occupy intermediate positions, with some suggestion that in the second and third generations problem drinking for Italian women is more serious than for Swedish women.

In the previous chapter hypothesis 1 stated that *frequency of nonabstainers would be as follows: Irish, Jewish, Italian, Swedish, English.* This hypothesis, however, turns out to be irrelevant since in the urban environment there are very few nonabstainers. One suspects that the English nonabstainers who depress the English drinking rate nationally are rural and Southern.

The English, as predicted, were the most frequent drinkers; the Swedish and the Italians intermediate, and the Jews the least frequent drinkers. Similarly, the Irish and the English drank the most at a single sitting, Swedes and Italians were intermediate, and Jews drank the least. The Irish and English were the most likely to have serious trouble with drinking, Italians and Jews the least likely (save for Italian women), and the Swedish were intermediate in their drinking problems. These findings persisted in both generations save for the fact that Irish teenagers were less likely to drink (though not less likely to have drinking problems) than other groups.

The only major change in the ordering of hypothesis 1 is that the Italians actually consume more alcohol than do the Swedes. Otherwise, our first prediction about drinking subcultures was confirmed by the evidence.

Most of the research done on religioethnic drinking patterns has indicated that English Protestant Americans are a relatively abstemious group compared to the Catholic ethnic immigrants. Data reported in these chapters, however, indicates heavy drinking and serious drinking problems among English Protestants. The probable explanation is that national sample data is heavily affected by rural and Southern Protestants— especially those of Baptist, Methodist, and Fundamentalist affiliation— and that our big-city sample has a relatively smaller proportion of such characteristically non-drinking Protestants than is to be found nationally. In Table 3.12 the Methodists and Baptists in our sample are compared with Jews at both adult and adolescent levels and appear to be relatively abstemious in comparison with other Protestants and with Catholic ethnic groups. Indeed, Methodist and Baptist adolescents drink less than Jewish adolescents and, while they are somewhat more likely to have serious drinking problems than Jewish adolescents, their score is still substantially below the mean. Adult Methodists and Baptists drink 22 ounces more a year of ethanol than Jews, but are still notably below the other ethnic groups, 23 standardized points below the mean in drinking problems. Thus, one can be reasonably confident that the heavy drinking of English Protestants noted in this report is an urban phenomenon based on the underrepresentation of Baptists and Methodists among urban Protestants.

TABLE 3.1

POWER AND SUPPORT IN ETHNIC FAMILIES

A. Parental-Adolescent Family

Power		Support	
Italian	.12	Italian	.15
Irish	.10	Jewish	.0
Swedish	-.12	Irish	.00
Jewish	-.30	Swedish	-.09

	Power	
	+	−
	Italian	Swedish
Support		
−Irish		
−Swedish		

B. Grandparental-Parent Family

Power		Support	
Jewish	.25	Jewish	.09
Italian	.09	Swedish	.07
Irish	.01	Irish	.00
Swedish	-.18	Italian	-.21

C. Efficacy Scores

Group	Score
Parents	
Jewish	.19
English	.11
Swedish	-.02
Irish	-.08
Italian	-.12
Adolescents	
Swedish	.11
Jewish	.09
English	-.01
Irish	-.04
Italian	-.07

TABLE 3.2

GRANDPARENTAL GENERATION DRINKING CULTURE (FROM LEFT TO RIGHT IN ORDER OF EXPECTED HEAVY DRINKING)

(per cent)

	Irish	Swedish	Italian	Jewish	English
Father drank twice a day or more	19	11	13	3	8
Father drank daily or more	46	46	48	15	33
Mother drank dialy or more	13	10	12	5	14
Parents always served drinks to guests	20	9	35	6	14
Drinking problem in home	40	30	13	4	21

TABLE 3.3

DRINKING BY ETHNIC GROUP BY SEX

	Ever Drink		Drink Now		Drink Almost Every Day or More		Predinner Drink Daily	
	Men	Women	Men	Women	Men	Women	Men	Women
Irish	100%	98%	89%	89%	48%	13%	35%	8%
Italian	100	99	95	91	40	11	21	3
Jewish	100	97	92	93	10	5	8	6
Swedish	100	93	89	89	31	9	22	6
English	97	97	97	90	45	18	37	12

	Heavy (moderate) Drinker		Would Miss Drinking A Lot (Some)		Age At First Drink (Yrs.)	
	Men	Women	Men	Women	Men	Women
Irish	11(74)%	1(31)%	19(54)%	7(15)%	19	20
Italian	6(53)	1(25)	6(34)	3(7)	18	20
Jewish	0(16)	1(21)	3(9)	4(8)	19	20
Swedish	6(67)	4(37)	12(42)	3(15)	19	22
English	11(68)	2(39)	9(41)	3(23)	20	21

Drinking Subcultures

TABLE 3.4

DRINKING OF SPECIFIC BEVERAGES BY ETHNIC GROUP

	Beer			
	3-4 Times a Week or More (%)		Amount in Bottles (Mean)	
	Men	Women	Men	Women
Irish	32	4	2.5	0.6
Italian	27	4	2.2	0.7
Jewish	0	0	0.9	0.4
Swedish	26	1	1.8	1.0
English	37	1	2.0	0.6

	Wine			
	1-2 Times a Week or More (%)		Amount in Glasses (Mean)	
	Men	Women	Men	Women
Irish	12	10	2.2	1.9
Italian	37	24	2.3	1.9
Jewish	18	17	2.5	1.2
Swedish	5	8	2.1	1.5
English	25	16	2.0	1.7

	Liquor			
	3-4 Times a Week or More (%)		Amount in Drinks (Mean)	
	Men	Women	Men	Women
Irish	20	7	2.2	1.9
Italian	20	4	2.2	1.8
Jewish	10	6	1.5	1.2
Swedish	23	9	2.1	1.5
English	16	14	2.0	1.8

TABLE 3.5

TOTAL ANNUAL ALCOHOL CONSUMPTION BY SEX, AGE, AND ETHNIC GROUP FOR ADULTS IN OUNCES OF ALCOHOL

	Irish	Italian	Jewish	Swedish	English
Men	388*(409**)	389 (547)	148 (346)	265 (268)	350 (345)
Women	124 (229)	133 (199)	90 (138)	139 (299)	144 (217)

Annual consumption of hard liquor ***

Men	153 (239)	144 (230)	103 (313)	152 (212)	132 (172)
Women	79 (192)	67 (137)	49 (104)	76 (168)	101 (195)

* Mean in total ounces.

** Standard deviation in total ounces.

*** Does not include beer or wine.

Ethnic Drinking Subcultures

TABLE 3.6

DRINKING "ENVIRONMENTS" OF ETHNIC GROUPS FOR ADULTS
(per cent)

	Drink Nearly Every Time Friends Get Together	More Than Half of Friends Drink a Lot	Usually Offer Drinks to Guests
Irish	54	30	75
Italian	41	24	78
Jewish	35	16	65
Swedish	36	23	61
English	44	28	67

Drinking Environment Scale by Ethnic Groups by Sex (Z Scores)

	Irish	Italian	Jewish	Swedish	English
Men	.36	−.09	−.43	.04	.17
Women	.00	−.13	−.20	−.27	.12

TABLE 3.7

DRINKING PROBLEMS AMONG AMERICAN ETHNIC GROUPS BY SEX FOR ADULTS
(% "Sometimes")

Questionnaire Item	Irish Men	Irish Women	Italian Men	Italian Women	Jewish Men	Jewish Women	Swedish Men	Swedish Women	English Men	English Women
I have difficulty walking straight after I have been drinking.	41	22	31	20	14	21	32	21	31	16
I have a hangover or severe headache after I have been drinking.	54	37	38	29	20	16	48	35	50	30
I fall asleep or pass out when I am drinking	19	3	16	16	6	13	15	7	14	6
I feel very sad when I am drinking.	17	19	18	23	8	14	9	17	12	11
Without realizing what I am doing I end up drinking more than I had planned to.	55	28	32	14	14	12	46	31	49	22
I don't nurse my drinks; I toss them down pretty fast.	47	15	33	9	37	17	47	17	44	15
Z Scores	.52	−.14	.14	−.05	−.25	−.34	.30	−.15	.38	−.28

Drinking Subcultures   49

TABLE 3.8A-B

ADOLESCENT DRINKING OF SPECIFIC BEVERAGES BY ETHNIC GROUP

	Beer			
	2-3 Times a Month or More (%)		Amount in Bottles (Mean)	
	Men	Women	Men	Women
Irish	28	18	1.9	1.4
Italian	29	23	2.1	1.2
Jewish	23	6	1.7	0.5
Swedish	23	19	1.8	1.2
English	36	21	2.5	1.5

	Wine			
	Once a Month or More (%)		Amount in Glasses (Mean)	
	Men	Women	Men	Women
Irish	11	11	0.7	1.0
Italian	17	17	0.9	0.8
Jewish	18	17	1.0	0.9
Swedish	7	12	0.7	1.0
English	15	19	0.9	0.8

	Liquor			
	Once a Month or More (%)		Amount in Drinks (Mean)	
	Men	Women	Men	Women
Irish	11	18	1.0	0.9
Italian	11	17	1.1	1.1
Jewish	8	11	0.8	0.5
Swedish	17	18	0.8	0.9
English	16	20	1.3	1.0

TABLE 3.8 A-B

ADOLESCENT DRINKING BY ETHNIC GROUP BY SEX

	% Ever Drink		Age at First Drink		% Drink 2-3 Times A Month or More		% High Once a Month or More	
	Boys	Girls	Boys	Girls	Boys	Girls	Boys	Girls
Irish	64	69	12.9	12.9	37	24	27	21
Italian	77	66	12.3	12.6	33	32	23	24
Jewish	79	70	12.3	13.5	26	22	20	15
Swedish	66	60	14.2	13.0	24	31	20	15
English	63	68	12.1	13.1	56	38	44	23
(All)			12.7	13.0				

Ethnic Drinking Subcultures

TABLE 3.9

TOTAL ANNUAL ALCOHOL CONSUMPTION FOR ADOLESCENT ETHNIC GROUPS BY
SEX (OUNCES OF ETHANOL)

	Irish	Italian	Jewish	Swedish	English
Boys	56	80	62	53	85
Girls	44	53	28	32	49

Mean Ounces of Ethanol Per Year of Hard Liquor Consumption by Adolescents by Ethnic Group by Sex.

	Irish	Italian	Jewish	Swedish	English
Boys	14	9	11	15	19
Girls	22	14	16	7	19

TABLE 3.10

ADOLESCENT DRINKING ENVIRONMENTS

% Saying Most or All Drink

	People in Your Grade	Close Friends
Irish	59	35
Italian	51	33
Jewish	46	30
Swedish	53	31
English	57	34

Drinking Environment Scores for Adolescents by Sex and Ethnic Group

	Irish	Italian	Jewish	Swedish	English
Boys	.12	.11	−.09	.03	−.04
Girls	.03	−.06	−.22	−.06	.01

Drinking Subcultures

TABLE 3.11

ADOLESCENT DRINKING PROBLEM BY SEX AND ETHNICITY
(Percent Sometimes)

Question: "There are many occasions, places or settings in which young people may drink beer, wine, or liquor. Indicate how frequently you drink beer, wine, or liquor in each setting...

	Irish Boys	Irish Girls	Italian Boys	Italian Girls	Jewish Boys	Jewish Girls	Swedish Boys	Swedish Girls	English Boys	English Girls
At teenage parties when others are drinking and your parents or other adults are not present	22	24	15	32	18	9	17	27	26	24
During or after a school activity such as a dance or football game when your parents or other adults you know are not present or can't see you	50	41	42	33	35	31	40	40	48	46
Driving around or sitting in a car at night	38	23	24	32	17	7	25	33	48	31
Alone	28	14	26	17	14	9	25	16	27	17
Z Scores *	11	-05	-06	10	-23	-38	-12	04	38	04

* Drinking alone and drinking in a car at night.

TABLE 3.12

BAPTIST AND METHODIST PROTESTANT AND JEWISH ALCOHOL CONSUMPTION AND DRINKING PROBLEMS BY AGE

	Adults	Adolescents
Baptist and Methodist Protestant		
Total alcohol (ounces)	149	32
Drinking problem (z scores)	-.23	-.15
Jews		
Total alcohol (ounces)	107	45
Drinking problem (z scores)	-.33	-.29

Ethnic Drinking Subcultures

CHAPTER FOUR
Explaining Drinking Subcultures

Having established the fact of a variety of drinking subcultures in all three generations, it is now appropriate to advance our "socialization" model for explaining ethnic variety (Table 4.1).

GENERAL MODELS

It is assumed that five different variables or sets of variables might influence a person's drinking behavior (or any ethnic-related behavior, for that matter): the behavior of one's parents, parental approval of the behavior in question, and the possibility of some kind of problem related to the behavior in the family of origin (Table 4.1). It is further assumed that the structure of the family in terms of POWER and SUPPORT might be influenced by parental drinking behavior and might in its turn influence respondent's drinking behavior. It is also assumed that various personality characteristics are susceptible to influence by family behavior and structure and in their turn will influence respondent's drinking. Another assumption is that a respondent's spouse's drinking may be influenced by respondent's family's drinking, family structure, and respondent's personality. (There may be aspects in the family of origin experience which predisposes one to select a spouse with similar predisposition.) Spouse's drinking will in turn influence one's own drinking. Finally, it is assumed that all four prior sets of variables may influence the drinking environment in which one finds oneself, and that in turn will influence one's own drinking.*

*The *family drinking scale* is composed of items that ascertain how much alcohol was consumed by father and mother, whether mother and father approved of people drinking, whether parents offered guests drinks in their home, and whether there was a drinking problem at home. The *family-structure variable* is composed of Power (how decisions were made in the family and how decisions about punishment of children for misbehavior were made) and Support (how close respondent was to each parent) measures. (These are the same scales that emerged in the secondary analysis of the 1971 Jennings political behavior material.) *Personality factors* in the personality scale are items that measure efficacy, attitudes toward authority and personal achievement. *Drinking environment* is composed of items that ascertain how often drinks are served at social occasions by the respondent's friends. *Spouse's* drinking is a composite score similar to the respondent's drinking scale.

Figure 4.1 is a path-analytic model which tests the assumptions in Table 4.1 for adult males. Two separate subsystems seem to be at work—a drinking "socialization" subsystem which affects both the amount consumed and the extent of drinking "problem" and a "personality" subsystem which relates only to drinking problems. Father's drinking affects the drinking environment in which an adult male lives as does parental approval of drinking. Mother's drinking, on the other hand, affects wife's drinking and also has a direct and powerful impact (beta = .24) on the amount of alcohol consumed per annum.

Whether a man who comes from a family where the mother drank is more likely to marry a wife who also drinks, or whether influenced by his mother he then influences his wife, is an issue which only extensive longitudinal research can answer. (Similarly, one may wonder if the father's drinking affects the choice of friends or whether one's own drinking, influenced by the father, leads one to choose drinking friends.) It seems reasonable to suspect, however, that the influences operate in both directions. For the present purposes, we assume the directionality indicated by Figure 4.1—fully aware of the complexities of husband-wife (or wife-husband) socialization which still must be sorted out in subsequent research.

Whatever the direction the linkage is between father and environment, between mother and wife, and between wife's drinking and friends' drinking influence, the amount consumed per year by an adult male and these three variables in their turn affect the likelihood that he will have a problem in his alcohol consumption. Problem drinking is also, as predicted, influenced by one's sense of personal efficacy and that in turn is influenced by the SUPPORT one experienced in one's family environment when growing up. Approximately a third of the variance in problem drinking is explained by the model and a quarter of the variance in total alcohol consumption.

There are both similarities and differences in the explanatory model for adolescent males. Mother's drinking continues to be a powerful predictor of the total amount consumed a year by an adolescent male. In fact the beta of .22 in figure 4.2 is virtually the same as the beta of .24 in Figure 4.1. Father's drinking has an indirect and relatively weak impact. (Mother's and father's drinking in Figure 4.2 are data taken directly from the parental questionnaire and not from retrospective questions.) However, the family structure/personality subsystem now is within the socialization system and not distinct from it and has a relatively minor impact through the peer-group drinking environment. Only the peer-group environment and the total amount consumed directly related to an adolescent's drinking-problem score. As was anticipated, the peer-group influence on adolescent drinking is enormous. Whether the model represented in Figure 4.1 will emerge more clearly in later years when the influence of the adolescent peer group diminishes remains to be seen. The similarities in the relative importance of maternal and paternal influence suggest, however, that the underlying dynamics of family socialization may not have changed for the younger generation. The most striking difference between the path-analytic diagram for adult women (Figure 4.3) and that for men is that the "structure/personality subsystem" is not distinct from the rest of the model. Furthermore the structural variable which influences women's drinking problems is power, not support and it affects problem drinking directly rather than indirectly through efficacy. Men from families where there was a lack of affection are more likely to drink while women from families with high concentration of power are more likely to drink. Furthermore while a problem in the family background did not seem to lead to a drinking problem for the adult men, there is a direct relationship between the two generations of problems for women. Indeed growing up in a family where there was a drinking problem (mostly the father's to judge by the correlation between frequency of father's drinking and family drinking problem) affects the drinking of the husband, and the drinking of friends but not the total consumption of alcohol. This suggests that we have made the right guess ordering the three variables the way we have. It would appear then that for a girl the experience of a drinking father has certain complications for her adult life which do not affect the boy raised in the same milieu.

Despite this phenomenon the principle influences on the amount a woman drinks are her mother and their friends, the husband exercising *his* influence just as do the wives, through the behavior of friends (and being substantially less important than friends). Indeed, the betas among mother, spouse, friends and own drinking are strikingly similar for both adult groups:

	Men	Women
Mother-self	.24	.18
Mother-environment	.10	not signif.
Mother-spouse	.16	.12
Spouse-environment	.18	.17
Spouse-self	.12	not signif.
Environment-self	.28	.33

The major differences in the men's and women's models pertain to problem drinking. Drinking of friends and total amount consumed have relatively the same affect on men and women, but low levels of support and consequently low feelings of efficacy lead to problem drinking among men, while growing up in a high power family and one where there is problem drinking, disposes a woman to have a drinking problem. In the next chapter we will see whether these patterns vary among different ethnic groups.

Among girls (Figure 4.4), the mother continues to have the stronger impact on drinking and, through her influence on drinking, to exercise also an impact on the presence of problem drinking on her daughters. Thus, the influence of the mother exists for both sexes (though, as we shall see subsequently, some ethnic groups are an exception). Otherwise, the two adolescent models are relatively the same, save that support has a much stronger role to play for girls than for boys. The direct and indirect paths from support to total amount consumed add to .10 for teenage women and the indirect paths (through environment and amount consumed between support and problem drinking add to .19. Family structure, then, is important for women in that it can directly or indireclty influence the possibility of drinking problems for them. For teenage women, however, it is the absence of affection in the family that leads them to drinking problems while for women it is the experience of growing up in a family where power was concentrated (and where there was a paternal drinking problem) that produces a propensity to have a drinking problem. This difference may represent a generationl change or merely a life-cycle variation. Teenage women may need immediate affection to avoid drinking problems, while older women are better able to avoid difficulties with drinking if they had the experience of growing up in a more democratic family environment.

By way of summary, in all of the groups the propensity to drink heavily is influenced most notably by the drinking behavior of mother and friends. For adults the spouse also plays a role, though not as important as friends. Drinking problems are influenced by efficacy for men, power and drinking problems in the family of origin for women, and support for girls (in addition to the direct effect of the amount consumed and the direct and indirect effects of environment and mother in all four groups). Personality and family structure variables play little role in the problem drinking of boys, yet as we shall see in the next chapter family structure has a very strong influence on the drinking behavior of Swedish adolescents.

Does our socialization/personality model account for the differences in drinking behavior among the various ethnic groups? In Table 4.2, we use a dummy-variable, multiple-regression technique to test the possibility that it does for amount consumed.

The Irish drink 127 ounces of ethanol a year more than Jews, Italians 136 ounces more, and the Swedes 91 ounces more.* When one takes into account mother's drinking and father's drinking, these differences are all substantially reduced to 95 ounces for the Irish, 98 ounces for Italians, and 65 ounces for Swedes. Thirteen more ounces are reduced from the Irish differential by taking into account spouse's drinking, 6 more from the

---

*Men and women are combined in this section of the analysis since the factors explaining alcohol consumption—as opposed to problem drinking—are basically similar, and the increase in the number of respondents makes a test of statistical significance possible.

Italian differential, and 10 from the Swedish. When the impact of drinking environment is added to the model, there are only 61 ounces of difference in ethanol consumption between the Irish and Jews, 92 ounces between Italians and Jews, and 55 ounces between Swedes and Jews. The difference between Italians and Jews is statistically significant at a confidence level of between 90 and 95 percent, while the differences between the Irish and Jews and Swedes and Jews are outside the 90 percent confidence interval. Our relatively simple model, then, based on mother's drinking, spouse's drinking, and drinking environment, reduces the sheer amount of alcohol consumption of Irish, Swedes, and Jews to levels that are not significant statistically.

The same assertions can be made regarding differences in hard liquor consumption (Table 4.3), though as far as the Irish, Italians, and Swedes are concerned, father, mother, and spouse account for most of the reduction in differences in hard liquor consumption between these three ethnic groups and Jews. Environment provides no additional explanatory power for the Irish-Jewish difference and the Italian-Jewish difference in intake of ethanol in hard liquor per year, and it only reduces the differences of the Swedes and the Jews 6 ounces and 11 ounces in the English-Jewish difference. For the four non-English groups, at any rate, hard liquor consumption differences are mostly a matter of the impact of mother, father, and spouse; differences in hard liquor consumption among those four groups, then, result from socialization in the family of origin and the family of procreation.

If one then adds to the model the religiousness of Jewish respondents*, virtually all the differences go away, though compared to unaffiliated reform Jews, Italians still drink 31 more ounces of ethanol per year. The differences in alcohol intake—as distinguished from differences in alcohol problems—among the four groups can be accounted for by the influence of mother, father, spouse, drinking environment, and Jewish religious tradition without any need to appeal to personality or family background, or genetic influences. The Irish drink more than Jewish adults, for example, because their fathers drink more, because their mothers drink more, because they are in a heavier drinking environment, and because religious Jews have a special attitude towards alcohol. In other words, as far as quantity of alcohol intake per year is concerned, one need not appeal to personality or family structure to explain the differences in drinking behavior.

Finally, even though the differences in alcohol are much smaller among adolescents than among adults, the same model continues to be effective in explaining the different levels of alcohol consumption, but Italians drink some 20 ounces more a year of ethanol than do Jews in the

---

*Following Snyder 1958, we use synagogue affiliations—orthodox and conservative versus reform and nonaffiliated.

adolescent generation. These differences are virtually eliminated when the socialization impact of mother, father, and environment are taken into account. As far as there are differences in alcohol consumption among ethnic groups, these differences can be explained both at the adolescent and the adult levels almost entirely in terms of family and environmental influence (and in the case of Jewish adults, religious influence.)

PROBLEM DRINKING

The socialization/personality model also accounts for most of the differences in "problem" drinking among the ethnic groups—without having to take into account their differential levels of alcohol consumption.

Men

Irish adult males are 78 standardized points higher than Jews on the problem-drinking scale, the Swedes 54 points higher, and the Italians 40 points higher (Table 4.5). The raw difference between Irish and Jews is diminished 10 points by taking into account the higher level of family drinking "problems" among the Irish and another 18 points by taking into account the higher drinking environment of Irish men.

In other words, a little more than one-third of the difference between Irish and Jewish men can be accounted for by differences in drinking problems in the family background and by the present drinking environment (Table 4.6). The differences between Italians and Jews is virtually eliminated, declining from 40 to 15 standardized points by taking into account family drinking problems, personality, and drinking environment. The difference between Swedes and Jews is diminshed from 54 to 33 points by taking into account the greater probability of a drinking problem in the Swedish family background and personality differences. Finally, when the comparison is made between the Gentile groups and those Jews who are not affiliated with synagogues or only with reformed synagogues, the remaining differences vanish completely.

Irish men are more likely to have drinking problems than Jewish men because they come from families where there are more likely to be drinking problems, because they live in a more heavy drinking environment, and because they lack the religious orientation toward alcohol that more traditional Jews have. There is no need, in other words, to appeal to either family structure or personality to explain the differences in drinking problems between Irish and Jews.*

---

*Even though many of the Irish are devout Roman Catholics and wine is used in the Catholic mass, wine does not have the sacred significance in the Catholic cultural/social tradition that it has in the Jewish tradition—in part, perhaps, because between the Council of Trent and the Second Vatican Council holy communion was taken in the Western Catholic Church only under the "species of bread."

There remains the question of the difference in drinking problems between the two Catholic groups. If Irish Catholics and Italian Catholics are compared with one another (Table 4.7), one observes that in a Catholic population the relative difference between Irish and Italians is 32 standardized points. If one takes into account that the Irish are more likely to have a family drinking problem, the difference is diminished by 9 points. The higher levels of SUPPORT in the Italian family diminish the difference 3 more points, and the lower propensity of Italians to enter heavy drinking environments accounts for virtually the remainder of the difference. Italians, in other words, are less likely to have drinking problems than the Irish because they are less likely to come from families with drinking problems and less likely to be in heavy drinking environments. There is no need to invoke personality differences to explain the different propensities to drinking problems; and the family-structure difference (Support) only makes a minor contribution to an explanation. Environmental influences, in other words, past and present, account for the difference in drinking problems between the Irish and Italians. Furthermore, if one examines Table 4.6, one notes that the differences between the Irish and the Jews, insofar as they can be accounted for by the model, do not relate to family structure or personality but rather to family drinking problems and drinking environment. The differences between the Irish and Italians and between the Irish and Jews can be accounted for without having to fall back on explanations of either family structure or personality.

Adult males from different ethnic groups have different propensities to be problem drinkers accounted for by the model elaborated at the beginning of the research project and the differences between the various groups can be considerably diminished, if not althogether eliminated, by taking into account environmental influences past and present and the special Jewish religious tradition. As we shall see in a subsequent chapter, however, different socialization dynamics are at work within the different ethnic collectivities, and in these dynamics matters of personality, and family structure are of considerable importance.

Boys

When one turns to drinking problems among adolescent males (Table 4.8), there is no need even to appeal to Jewish religiousness. The Irish raw difference of 34 from the Jews is reduced to 26 when mother's drinking is taken into account, to 18 when support is taken into account, to 16 when efficacy is taken into account, and to an insignificant 5 when environment is taken into account (Table 4.9). Thus, even though family structure and personality do not explain the differences between Irish and Jewish adult men, they are important in explaining some of the differences between Irish and Jewish boys. A difference of 26 when mother's drinking is taken into account is reduced 11 points when one considers that Irish adolescent males come from a less supportive family environment than the Jews and that their feelings of personal efficacy are lower. Support also reduces by 5 points the 17-point difference between Italians and Jews, and that difference is reduced 7 points further when the higher Italian drinking environment is taken into account. The model also eliminates entirely the difference between the Italians and the Irish—principally through a higher support in the Italian family and a higher drinking environment in the Irish family than in the Italian family. The relatively small 10-point raw difference between Swedes and Jews is affected principally by the mother's drinking and by drinking environment. Differences between the two Catholic groups and Jews involve family structure and, in the case of the Irish, also personality. The difference between Swedes and Jews is more one of environment—that provided by the mother and by the adolescent peer group.

Women

The differences among women in drinking follow the same pattern as those among men, but the magnitude is not nearly so great (Table 4.10). The importance of parental drinking in explaining the drinking problems of women are especially clear when we attempt to reduce the raw differences between the four Gentile groups and the Jews among adult males (Table 4.11). When parental drinking is taken into account, all differences between Italian and Jewish women are eliminated, and when parental approval is taken into account, the differences between Swedish and English women and Jews are eliminated. The differences between the Irish and Jews are unaffected, however, by parental drinking and are reduced by a combination of parental approval of drinking and education. (The better educated an Irish and Jewish woman is the less likely she is to drink, and Jewish women are somewhat better educated than Irish.) Differences are eliminated completely when the difference in drinking environment is taken into account.

Girls

The general model when applied to young women is much less successful in diminishing the differences between Jews and Gentiles (See Tables 4.12 and 4.13). The difference between the Irish and Jews is reduced from 33 points to 19 points, efficacy being the most important of the variables. The difference between Italians and Jews is reduced from 48 to 36 points, again with efficacy being the most important variable. The difference between Swedes and Jews is reduced from 39 to 30 points with efficacy accounting for the greatest decline. The difference is reduced from 39 to 30 points for the English too, but parental approval is the most powerful explanatory factor. Thus, the fact that Jewish women have higher feelings of personal efficacy than do Irish, Italian, and Swedish women is the principal explanation available to us for the different levels of drinking problems among Jews and Gentiles.

If one then turns to the Jewish religiousness factor, we have considerably more success. Eighteen Jewish women, either unaffiliated or belonging to reform congregations were in our sample. The differences between them and the Irish approach zero when the other variables in the model are taken into account, and the difference between the Jewish young women and the Swedes and the English declines to 13 points. The difference between Jewish and Italian young women declines to 20 points. A combination of the general model and Jewish religiousness seems to account for most of the difference in drinking problems between Jewish young women and Gentile young women, and all of the difference when the comparison is with the Irish (See Table 4.14). Interestingly enough, we have had to appeal to the Jewish religiousness explanation for men and for girls. We must speculate about the reasons for this interaction between religiousness and sex. It may be that in the short run, during the troubled years of adolescence, religious affiliation has a more critical effect on drinking behavior for Jewish women than it does for men, but over the long run, as the life cycle smooths out, religious affiliation is more important for men than for women. It is also possible, however, that we are dealing with a generational rather than a life cycle model, and that young Jewish women find themselves caught in more serious temptations to depart from the traditional Jewish norms of women's drinking behavior and hence are more likely to be affected by their style of religious affiliation. Only subsequent research on this generation of Jewish adolescent women in adult life will reveal the answer to this question.

CONCLUSION

Thus, we can conclude this chapter with the observation that three of our basic assumptions have been partially or totally confirmed by the data.

1. There are indeed problem-drinking subcultures that differ among various ethnic groups. These differences tend to persist, though with some exceptions, across both generational and sex lines.
2. General models can be devised, especially when they take into account Jewish religiousness, that eliminate or notably reduce the variety in problem drinking among the various groups.
3. We also suggested on the basis of previous NORC research that problem drinking among English Amercans who did drink might be even higher than that of problem drinking among Irish Catholics. This proposition was not sustained for women and both young men and young women. While it is surely true, then, that the Irish are heavy drinkers and

more prone to have serious drinking problems than any of the other immigrant groups studied, it is not true that they are any more prone to serious drinking problems than northern urban Americans whose ancestors migrated from Great Britain.

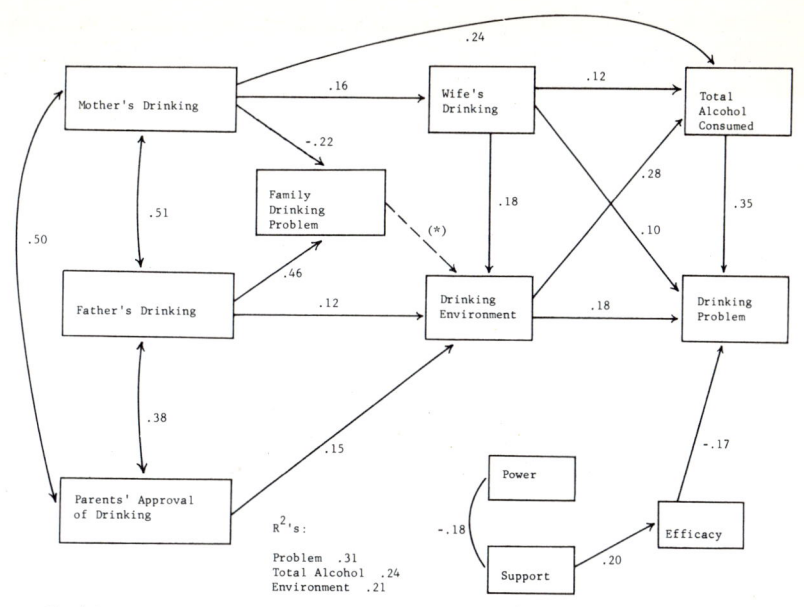

Fig. 4.1 --Drinking Model for Adult Males*

*Only relationships larger than .07 are shown.

R²'s:
Problem   .31
Total Alcohol   .24
Environment   .21

TABLE 4.1

GENERAL MODEL TO EXPLAIN ETHNIC DRINKING BEHAVIOR

Family Drinking	Family Structure	Personality Scale	Spouse's Drinking	Drinking Environment
Fequency (mother, father)	POWER			
Approval	SUPPORT			
Family drinking problem when growing up		Efficacy		

Explaining Drinking Subcultures   63

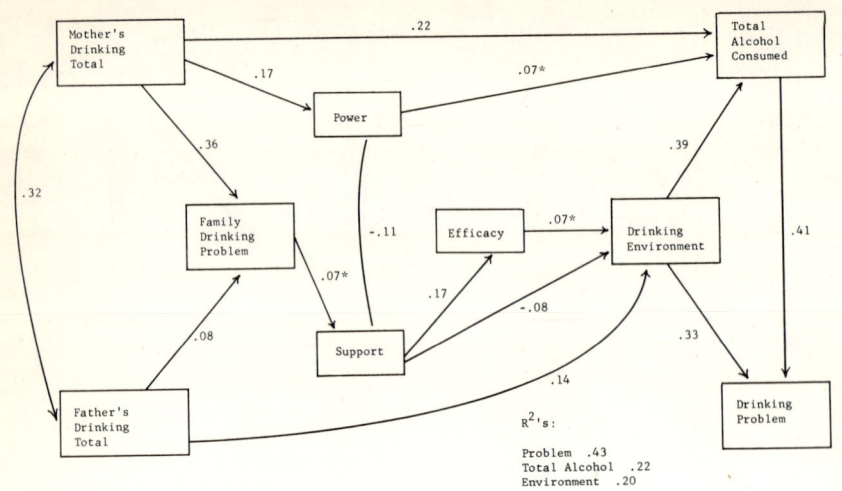

Fig. 4.2 -- Drinking Model for Adolescent Males*

R^2's:
Problem .43
Total Alcohol .22
Environment .20

*Only relationships larger than .07 are shown.

TABLE 4.2

MODEL TO EXPLAIN DIFFERENCES IN TOTAL ALCOHOL
CONSUMPTION OF ADULTS
(Differences in ounces of ethanol from Jews)

	Irish	Italian	Swedish	English
Raw difference	17	136	91	126
Mother's drinking	113	116	77	110
Father's drinking	95	98	65	108
Spouse's drinking	82	92	55	97
Environment	61*	92**	55*	73**
Unaffiliated or reform Jews	00	31	00	00

* B is outside the 90% confidence interval.

** B is between the 90% and the 95% confidence interval.

64   *Ethnic Drinking Subcultures*

Figure 4.3

DRINKING MODEL FOR ADULT WOMEN *

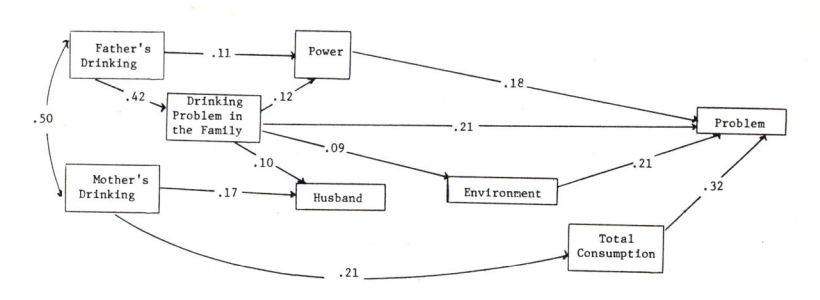

*Only relationships larger than .07 are shown here.

R^2
Problem = .27
Total Alcohol = .17
Environment = .09

TABLE 4.3

MODEL TO EXPLAIN DIFFERENCES FROM JEWS IN OUNCES OF HARD LIQUOR CONSUMED BY ADULTS

	Irish	Italian	Swedish	English
Raw difference	44	34	46	48
Mother's drinking	38	25	41	42
Father's drinking	29	17	34	41
Spouse's drinking	10	12	27	32
Environment	10	12	21	21

Explaining Drinking Subcultures 65

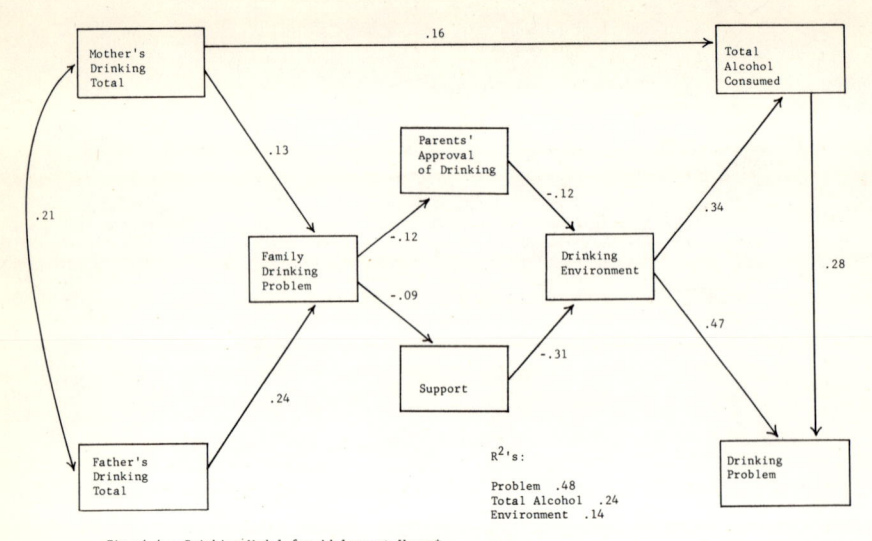

Fig. 4.4 -- Drinking Model for Adolescent Women*

*Only relationships greater than .09 are shown.

TABLE 4.4

MODEL TO EXPLAIN DIFFERENCES IN TOTAL ALCOHOL CONSUMPTION
FOR ADOLESCENTS
(Differences in Total Ounces)

	Irish	Italian	English
Raw difference	4	20	20
Mother's drinking	0	16	14
Father's drinking	0	14	12
Environment	0	06	07

TABLE 4.5

DRINKING PROBLEMS FOR ADULT MALES

	Irish	Italian	Jewish	Swedish	English	All
Male parents (z score on problem drinking scale*)	52	14	-25	30	38	29

* The mean is zero for the whole population including women.

66   *Ethnic Drinking Subcultures*

TABLE 4.6

DIFFERENCES FROM JEWISH ADULTS IN DRINKING PROBLEM SCORE
(Standardized points)

	Men Irish	Italian	Swedish	English
Raw difference	78	40	54	63
Family drinking problem	68	36	45	62
POWER	68	36	37	62
Personality	68	29	37	62
Drinking environment	50	15	33	33
Jewish Religion	00	00	00	00
Percent of difference eliminated by model	100	100	100	100

TABLE 4.7

EXPLANATION BY GENERAL MODEL OF DIFFERENCES BETWEEN IRISH
AND ITALIAN MEN IN DRINKING PROBLEM
(Standardized points)

Raw difference	32
Family drinking problem	23
SUPPORT	20
Drinking environment	05

* Analysis limited to two Catholic ethnic groups.

TABLE 4.8

DRINKING PROBLEMS FOR ADOLESCENT MEN

(Z score--from total adolescent population mean)

Irish	Italian	Jewish	Swedish	English	All
+11	-06	-23	-12	+38	-03

Explaining Drinking Subcultures 67

TABLE 4.9

EXPLANATION OF DIFFERENCES FROM JEWS IN DRINKING PROBLEMS
OF ADOLESCENT MEN OF OTHER ETHNIC GROUPS

	Irish	Italian	Swedish	English
Raw difference	34	17	10	61
Mother's drinking (total ounces)	26	17	06	55
SUPPORT	18	12	04	43
Efficacy	15	12	04	43
Drinking environment	05	05	00	40

TABLE 4.10

DRINKING PROBLEMS FOR ADULT WOMEN
(Z scores--from total population mean)

Irish	Italian	Jewish	Swedish	English	All
-14	-05	-34	-15	-28	-22

TABLE 4.11

DRINKING PROBLEM MODELS FOR ADULT WOMEN
(Betas)

Explanation by general model of differences in drinking between jews and gentile ethnic groups fpr adult women.

	Irish	Italian	Swedish	English
Raw difference	24	16	21	09
Parental drinking	24	00	07	09
Parental approval of drinking	15	xx	00	00
Education	10	xx	xx	xx
Environment	00	xx	xx	xx

Note: xx model has already explained the difference.

TABLE 4.12

DRINKING PROBLEM FOR ADOLESCENT WOMEN
(Z score from total adolescent mean)

Irish	Italain	Jewish	Swedish	English	ALL
-.05	.10	-.38	.04	.04	-.03

TABLE 4.13

Explanation by general model of differences between Jews and gentile ethnic groups for adolescent women.

	Irish	Italian	Swedish	English
Raw difference	33	48	39	39
Mother's Drinking (total ounces)	30	47	36	39
SUPPORT	30	47	36	39
Efficacy	21	40	31	36
Parental approval	19	36	30	30
Religiousness of Jewish adolescent women *	00	20	13	13

* Score of unaffiliated or reform members (n=18).

TABLE 4.14

STANDARD DEVIATIONS ON DRINKING PROBLEM SCALES FOR IRISH
AND JEWISH ETHNIC GROUPS BY GENERATION AND SEX
(Z scores)

	Adults		Adolescents	
	Men	Women	Boys	Girls
Irish	1.22	.93	1.04	.93
Jewish	.74	.65	.89	.75

Explaining Drinking Subcultures 69

CHAPTER FIVE
Socialization Subcultures

Ethnic differences not only exist, then, they perdure. And they not only perdure, but they can be explained by "socialization"—mostly insofar as the variety in which what parents (especially the mother), spouse, and friends do is far more important than what they say. It is unlikely that parents deliberately train their young people to be, let us say, "Irish" drinkers, much less to have "Irish" drinking problems. Ethnic subcultures seem to get passed on more by unconscious imitation than by conscious design.

There is also the possibility that the dynamics of socialization may vary from group to group. Ethnic subcultures may involve not only different outcomes but also different processes. Operationally, this possibility may be reduced to the question of whether the path models in Figures 5.1 and 5.2 may vary from group to group. In terms of statistical inference, the question is whether there are "significant" interactions with ethnicity in the model.

A method to test for interactions was developed by Christian W. Jacobsen of the NORC staff using saturated models; since theoretical beliefs implied interethnic group differences in the models, factor (ethnic group) by covariate (independent variable) interaction effects needed to be considered in the restriction process.

For each dependent variable in turn, the general saturated model consisted of all causally prior covariates, the ethnic group factor, and their attendant factor by covariate interaction effects. Effects restriction was accomplished by backward elimination with no covariate removed from the equation unless its factor by covariate interaction term had been already eliminated. In order to insure that the effects retained were independent of intergroup differences in covariate means, the ethnic-group factor was never eliminated. Analysis of covariance employing a regression partitioning of the sums of squares was used for this purpose with the criterion for termination being the .10 alpha level as determined by the F-test.

This process often resulted in mixed-effects equations with some covariate effects varying across ethnic groups, and others not. The resulting path diagrams and decompositions are, therefore, conditional path models showing the effects implied by the mixed effects equations when each of the ethnic groups is considered by itself. That is, some path coefficients vary across diagrams for a given model specification; others do not. The same holds true for the decomposition of effects. In other words, those additive relationships remaining that had "lost" their interactive counterpart were "restricted"—not permitted to vary in a "restricted" model from which direct and indirect paths for each ethnic group were computed. Figures 5.3 and 5.4 represent the "restricted" models for adult males and adolescent males.

There are, then, many intricate interactions with ethnicity in all the models. For the purposes of the present study, however, it is sufficient to examine those interactions that have a notable impact on alcohol consumption and on drinking "problems." Such interactions establish the fact of different socialization processes working among the various groups and indicate the nature of these different processes.

MEN

The principal ethnic interactions with alcohol consumption for adult males involve the drinking of the two "women in their lives"—mother and wife (Table 5.1). Wife's drinking is of medium importance for the three non-Catholic groups, of no importance for Italians, and of considerable importance for the Irish. Mother's drinking, on the other hand, is of considerable importance for the Italians, of medium importance for the two Protestant groups, and of lesser importance for the Irish and Jews. To view the matter from a different perspective, the Irish and Jews have a culture in which the wife is substantially more important than the mother in her influence on drinking behavior, the Swedes and the English have a culture in which they are of approximately equal importance, and the Italians have a culture in which the mother is important and the wife of no importance in their respective effect on an adult male's drinking. (So much for the myth of the all-powerful Jewish and Irish mother—at least as far as drinking is concerned.)

The wife and mother interactions are important also in their impact on the drinking-problem scale. The strongest relationship between "problems" and the drinking of the wife is for the Swedes. There is almost no relationship between wife's drinking and problems for the Italians and Irish and a *negative* relationship between wife's drinking and drinking "problems" for Jews. Similarly, mother's drinking has a higher influence on drinking problems for Swedish, English, and Italian men, a small influence on Irish men, and a negative influence on Jewish men.

Thus, drinking of the "women in their lives" is most important in effecting the drinking problems of the two Protestant groups, modestly important for the two Catholic groups, and negatively related to drinking problems for Jewish men. If Irish and Italian men turn to problem drinking, the alcohol consumption of their mothers and wives seems to be unrelated to the phenomenon. Perhaps the Jewish men with wives and mothers who drink little are more likely to have drinking problems because their drinking represents a turn away from their family and religious culture—a turning away which has all the more negative impact precisely because it is done alone.

For three of the groups there is the expected negative relationship between problem drinking and parental disapproval of drinking. The English group has no such relationship (suggesting perhaps the breakdown of an older Protestant nondrinking subculture). But among the Swedes it is precisely those who come from strongly disapproving backgrounds who are the most likely to have high drinking-problem scores—perhaps as part of an alienating revolt against a stern Swedish Lutheran background.

The personality subsystem has little effect on problem drinking for the two Protestant ethnic groups. But both the "high-problem" Irish Catholics and the "low-problem" Jews show strong negative relationships between "problem" drinking and efficacy and support. Thus, David McClellan's (1972) findings about low levels of affection and resulting low levels of self-esteem (and marked needs for power) are spectacularly confirmed for the Irish; and the previous research comparing the different family cultures and structures of the Irish and Jews and the relationship of these differences to problem drinking is also replicated. As we pointed out earlier, however, one does not need to take into account these personality and structural differences to account for the different problem levels between Irish and Jews. Both groups are affected in their drinking by family structure and personality but all of the differences in drinking can be accounted for by the fact that Irish grow up in families, form families, and associate in friendship groups where more drinking occurs.

By way of brief summary, the Swedish and English male problem-drinking subculture is heavy on the woman or socialization influence and light on the personality/family structure influence, while Jews, Irish and, to some extent, Italians are just the opposite—light (or even negative) on the "woman" influence and heavy on the personality influence. For both amount consumed and drinking problems there are significantly different drinking subcultures among the groups being studied—different processes as well as different outcomes.

BOYS

There are also notable differences in the processes for male adolescents though some of them seem to be the opposite of the processes for male adults, perhaps because of the disproportionate influence of the peer-group environment on adolescent drinking and the strikingly large interaction between ethnicity and peer-group influence both on amount consumed and drinking problems (Table 5.2). Environment has the strongest impact for the Protestant groups, an intermediate impact for Jews and Italians, and lowest for the Irish. On the other hand, the sheer amount consumed has the strongest impact on the two Catholic groups, an intermediate impact on Jews, and the lowest impact on Protestant adolescents. An Irish, Italian, or Jewish teenage boy, in other words, is less likely than his Protestant counterpart to be tempted into problem drinking by his friends and more likely to get into problem drinking by reason of the sheer amount consumed.

The only family structural variable which interacts for adolescents is POWER, and then only with amount consumed. Protestant adolescent men from authoritarian families are more likely to drink. There is no such relationship in the non-Protestant group.

It is in comparing the mother's impact on drinking in both generations that we encounter the greatest complexity. For the two Protestant groups the mother has a notable impact on both the amount consumed and problems for adults, but she has no impact worth noting for adolescents. Could it be that in both the Swedish and English groups the cross-generational influence is weakening in the face of a peer group environmental influence? Or might it be rather that when the peer-group influence fades, the maternal influence will reassert itself?

Among the three non-Protestant groups, however, there is a rough replication of the pattern of the previous generation; Italian mothers have more impact on the drinking behavior of their sons than do Jewish or Irish mothers. But Jewish mothers of teenage sons are at present having more effect on the behavior of their offspring than did Jewish mothers of an earlier generation on the behavior of Jewish adult males. Finally, in both generations women's drinking (as opposed to their affection) has little influence in the drinking problems of Irish males.

There is also an ethnic interaction between efficacy and drinking environment which is lost in the restrictive model but which emerges in a simple three-variable model of support, efficacy, and environment for adolescent males; but, to keep to the rules of the inference game, we must report it as "unproven": Irish, .15; Italian, .24; Jewish, .20; Swedish, .04; English, .08. Non-Protestant adolescent males with low feelings of self-esteem are more likely than their Protestant counterparts to be in a heavy drinking environment. This tendency bears observing if continued research with the same population is possible.

Thus, in both generations of men there are different outcomes of drinking socialization and different processes. The principal differences have to do with the importance of the influence of the drinking of relevant women and with the importance of personality influences (especially if parental disapproval is considered a personality-related factor for the

Swedes. The presence of the enormous peer group influence in the teenage generation makes it impossible to assert that the various groups have similar models for both the grandparent/parent and the parent/teenager socialization encounter, but at least among the three non-Protestant groups there seems to be some rough similarity.

WOMEN

The only interaction with ethnicity and total amount of alcohol consumed is with the mother's drinking, with the correlations being high for Jews and Swedes and low for the Irish and Italians (Table 5.3). The high relationship for Swedes and the low one for Italians parallels the interaction for adult men. The interactions with drinking problems for adult women, however, are completely different from those for men: drinking problems in the family of origin and the father's drinking. For both variables the correlation is highest for the Irish (.31 and .16, respectively). The father's drinking correlation is trivial for other groups; and even for the Irish it exercises its influence indirectly through problem drinking in the family. Problem drinking in the family has a moderate relationship with a woman's own drinking problem for Swedes and a negative relationship for Italians. Irish and Swedish women with problem drinking in their background are likelier themselves to be problem drinkers, while Italian women with the same background are less likely to be problem drinkers, perhaps because in the Italian culture there is little sympathy for the alcoholic male and, hence, little propensity for a daughter to sympathize with and imitate her father's behavior. It is worth noting that the only relationship between the father's drinking and one's own drinking recorded in this study is for Irish adult women and then only because of that drinking having become a drinking problem.

The folklore of alcoholism speaks of drinking problems being passed on from generation to generation. Our evidence, hardly conclusive, indicates that this happens only for Swedish and Irish women.

Father's drinking and drinking problems in the family lead to problem drinking for adult women. Problem drinking in the family also affects Swedish women and English women, though the latter less so. Neither the Jews nor the Italians are affected by either background variable.

GIRLS

Mother's drinking affects daughter's drinking for adolescent women more powerfully for the non-Catholic groups than for the Catholic groups—a replication of the finding for adult women (Table 5.4). Indeed, the relationship between mother's and daughter's drinking for Swedes is enormous (and represents a correlation between two questionnaires, not two answers on the same questionnaire.) There is also a substantial relationship between parental approval of girl's drinking and liquor consumed for Italians, possibly because of the strong ties of Italian family life in which approval or disapproval has a powerful impact on a young woman.

Finally, the absence of support has the strongest impact on the development of drinking problems for Irish and Swedish girls. Neither mother's drinking not total amount of alcohol consumed affects problem drinking for the Irish, while total consumed is a powerful predictor for other groups, and mother's drinking a moderate predictor for Jewish and English girls and a powerful predictor for Swedish girls.

Note that in both sexes and both generations the mother has little impact on problem drinking for the Irish; that it affects Italian men but not Italian women; that it affects Jewish young people but not adults; Swedish and English adult men and adolescent women. There is no better summary of the argument that there are different processes of drinking socialization among the various ethnic groups: there are four different patterns of maternal influence on problem drinking.

Indeed, there are enough interactions with ethnicity in the drinking socialization model to delight the most enthusiastic pluralist. One might illustrate the variety by imagining someone in the helping professions working with a client with an alcohol problem and wondering about the impact of the mother's drinking on the person. If the client was Irish, the helping person could assume that the mother's alcohol consumption was not part of the socialization process. If the person was an Italian man, the helping professional would have to be alert to the maternal influence, but would not need to be concerned about an Italian woman. Nor would one have to worry if the client was a Jewish adult or a Swedish or English boy. On the other hand, one would have to watch for the maternal drinking influence on the problem of the client if the client was a Jewish young person or a Swedish or English man or girl. In short, for the helping professional, the question of the mother's drinking influencing a drinking problem of her child can be dismissed for adult women. For other clients, the professional must ask questions about ethnic group, sex, and age to know whether to consider the maternal influence.

It is also worth noting that there is no evidence of a genetic transmission of drinking problems. Only Irish women are heavily influenced by a drinking problem in their father and they do not seem to pass this on to their sons. (Obviously, our data are not a definite answer to the genetic issue, especially since only those at the high end of our drinking-problem scale can be thought of as coming close to alcoholism in the traditional sense of the term.)

PARTIALING THE VARIANCE EXPLANATION

Another approach to the question of ethnic drinking subcultures is to partial out the relative impact of family of origin, present family and friendship groups, sheer amount of alcohol consumed, and personality/family structure on problem drinking. How much of our explanation of the problem drinking behavior of each group (adults for the sake of simplicity and convenience) can be accounted for without appealing to personality/family structure variables?

One may do this (Table 5.5) by examining the amount of variance explained by adding successive blocks of variables, adding first those that pertain to the family of origin; second, those that account for the present drinking of wife (husband) and friends; third, those taking into account the actual drinking behavior of the respondent; and fourth, those that add to the behavioral variables, the family structure and personality variables.

The model explains .45 of the variance in problem drinking among Irish males. The family of origin block contributes .14 variance explanation (31 percent of the total explanation). Present family and friends adds only .03 more explanation (together with family of origin present and family friends account for 38 percent of the total explanation). Amount consumed adds .15 more explanation and .13 additional explanation (29 percent of the total) is added by the personality block of variables. In other words, it is the family of origin, the amount consumed and the personality factors which—in approximately equal proportion—provide our explanation of Irish male problem drinking. One can see for the men that the model containing these variables differs considerably in its explanatory power for the various groups—explaining more than half the variance in Italian men's problem drinking, approximately two-fifths of the problem drinking variance for Irish and Swedes, a third of the variance among the Jews and only a fifth among the English.

Looking at the next to the bottom row, we see that the amount consumed (as we have measured it) adds little to the variance explained for Italian and Swedish men, but substantial amounts for the Irish, Jewish and English men. Even though the model explains much more of the Irish drinking variance than it does for the other two groups, within the respective explanations the family structure/personality account for substantial amounts of explanatory power in all of the ethnic groups.

It is also interesting to note that the behavior of present family and friends adds little explanatory power to the Irish model, but substantial amounts to all the others; Irish male drinking problems then are relatively independent of the behavior of present associates and, rather, are shaped by drinking in the family of origin and personality constellations shaped by that family.

The same observations can be made of Irish women in Table 5.5. They are like Jewish women relatively uninfluenced by present family and friends and moderately influenced by family structural variables, while the two Protestant groups are uninfluenced by family structure and notably influenced by the behavior of present associates, and Italians are influenced mostly by sheer amount of alcohol consumed. For both men and women then the Jews and the Irish are the most likely to be affected by their origins—the drinking behavior in their family and the personalities they acquired in the family environment; even though the Irish are the most likely to have serious drinking problems and the Jewish the least likely, the patterns of explanation are roughly similar.

It may well be, of course, that there are personality factors that affect the drinking of Italians and Swedes (of both sexes), but they are not the same ones that our measures tap among the Irish and Jews. A helping professional would have to be very conscious of the efficacy (for men) and power (for women) dimensions of his or her client's case. But if she or he was seeing next an Italian or Swedish client, expectations for the personality dimensions of the person's alcohol involvement would have to be considerably modified.

CONCLUSION

To recapitulate the last three chapters, we have found distinctive and durable drinking cultures among the various ethnic groups, we have been able to account for most of the differences in both alcohol consumed and problem drinking by a general explanatory model, and we have discovered that there is substantial ethnic variety in the drinking-socialization processes in the different subcultures, so much so that helping professionals would labor under a very great handicap if they are unaware of these differences. We have, however, only been able to offer tentative speculations about the reasons for the differences in socialization process, mostly because the study of variety in ethnic family structures is still in its infancy. The work of McClellan and Stivers and others provides a ready theoretical perspective to explain the enormous importance of support and efficacy for Irish men. But we have to fall back on thin speculation about an Irish woman's sympathy with and unconscious imitation of her father's problem drinking. We have also speculated about a Protestant revolt against older nondrinking cultures and about the impact of problem drinking in the nondrinking Italian and Jewish communities. These and all the other speculations are necessarily tentative. However, having established that family-structure differences are important at least for drinking problems, we have offered some reason for the scholarly community to re-examine these ethnic phenomena the demise of which seems to have been prematurely reported. How premature we will see in a subsequent chapter.

Figure 5.1

RESTRICTED MODEL FOR ADULT MALE DRINKING *

*Parameter not permitted to vary = ————————
Parameter permitted to vary = —————————

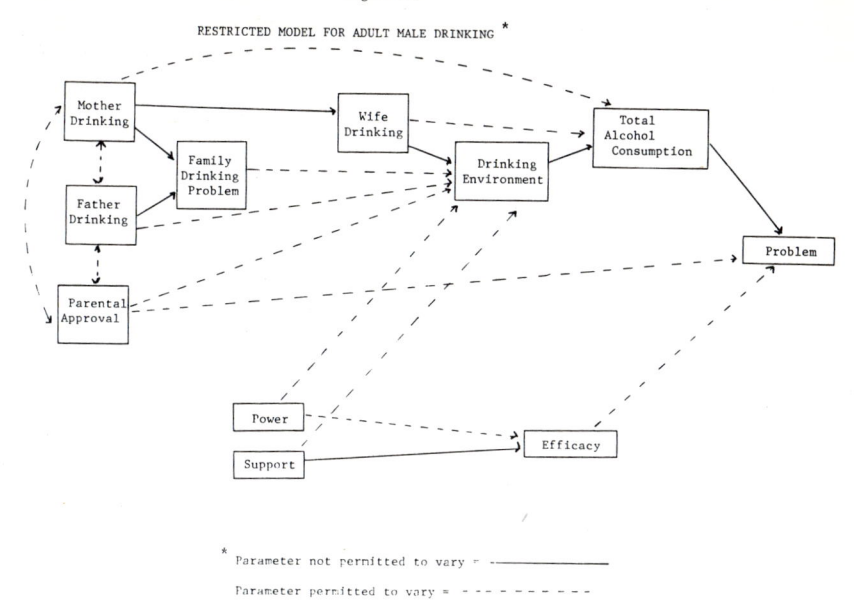

TABLE 5.1

PRINCIPLE INTERACTIONS WITH ETHNICITY IN DRINKING MODEL
(DIRECT AND INDIRECT PATHS FOR ADULT MEN)

A. Dependent Variable: Total Alcohol Consumed Per Year

	Irish	Italian	Jewish	Swedish	English
Wife's drinking	.36	-.09	.29	.26	.23
Mother's drinking	.14	.38	-.01	.28	.28

B. Dependent Variable: Drinking Problem Scale

	Irish	Italian	Jewish	Swedish	English
Wife's drinking	.08	.06	-.21	.44	.16
Mother's drinking	.05	.12	-.05	.17	.10
Parental disapproval of drinking	-.21	-.14	-.15	.31	-.01
SUPPORT	-.15	-.04	-.09	.09	-.02
Efficacy	-.37	-.14	-.27	-.01	-.01

Socialization Subcultures   79

Figure 5.2

RESTRICTED MODEL FOR ADOLESCENT MALE DRINKING *

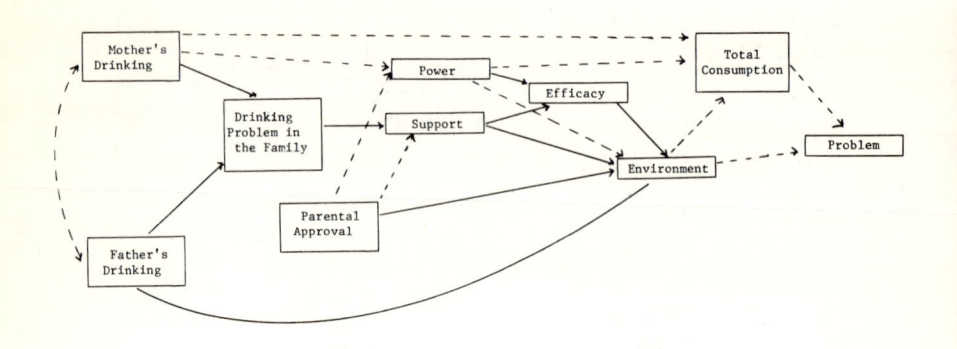

* Parameter not permitted to vary = ————————
  Parameter permitted to vary = – – – – – – –

TABLE 5.2

PRINCIPLE INTERACTIONS WITH ETHNICITY IN DRINKING MODEL
(DIRECT AND INDIRECT PATHS FOR ADOLESCENT MEN)

A. Dependent Variable: Total Alcohol Consumed Per Year

	Irish	Italian	Jewish	Swedish	English
Mother's drinking	.05	.60	.26	-.09	-.08
POWER	.04	-.06	-.05	.37	-.25
Drinking environment	.23	.46	.44	.45	.51

B. Dependent Variable: Drinking Problem Scale

	Irish	Italian	Jewish	Swedish	English
Mother's drinking	.03	.34	.13	-.03	.00
Environment	.24	.35	.53	.69	.59
Total drinking per year	.57	.58	.50	.25	.32

80 *Ethnic Drinking Subcultures*

Figure 5.3

RESTRICTED MODEL FOR ADULT WOMEN*

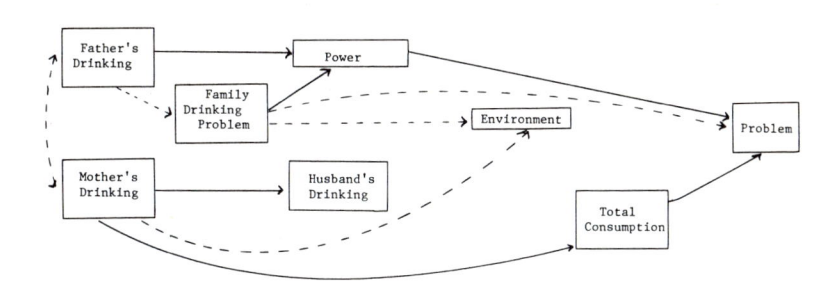

*Parameter not permitted to vary = ─────────

Parameter permitted to vary = ─ ─ ─ ─ ─ ─ ─

TABLE 5.3

INTERACTION FOR ADULT WOMEN

A. Dependent Variable: Total Alcohol Consumed Per Year

	Irish	Italian	Jewish	Swedish	English
Mother's drinking	.18	.18	.24	.31	.25

B. **Dependent Variable: Drinking Problem**

	Irish	Italian	Jewish	Swedish	English
Problem in family	.31	-.14	.01	.19	.10
Father's drinking	.16	-.03	.01	.09	.02

TABLE 5.4

INTERACTIONS FOR ADOLESCENT WOMEN

A. Dependent Variable: Total Alcohol Consumed Per Year

	Irish	Italian	Jewish	Swedish	English
Mother's drinking	-.11	-.09	.24	.90	.20
Parent approval	.02	.23	-.10	.12	.13

B. Dependent Variable: Drinking Problem

	Irish	Italian	Jewish	Swedish	English
Mother's drinking	-.01	-.04	.15	.37	.10
Total consumed	.09	.50	.62	.41	.50
Support	-.25	.01	-.13	-.56	-.13

Socialization Subcultures

Figure 5.4

RESTRICTED MODEL FOR ADOLESCENT WOMEN*

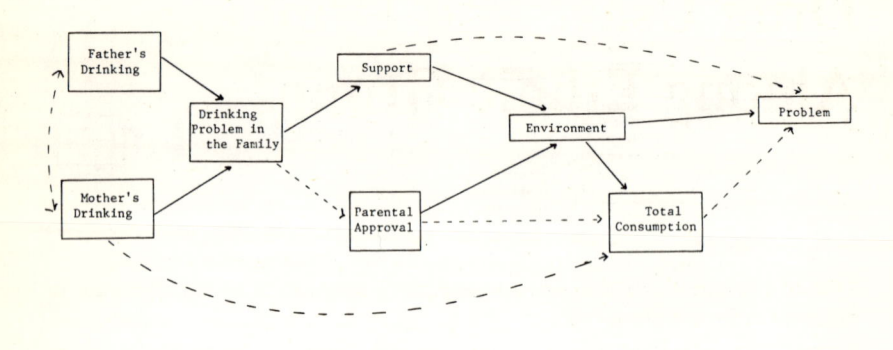

* Parameter not permitted to vary = ——————

Parameter permitted to vary = – – – – – – –

TABLE 5.5

PARTIAL EXPLANATIONS OF PROBLEM DRINKING

A. Men

	Irish r^2	Irish %	Italian r^2	Italian %	Jewish r^2	Jewish %	Swedish r^2	Swedish %	English r^2	English %
Family of origin*	.14	31	.19	37	.10	29	.20	50	.05	26
Present family and friends	.17	38	.32	62	.15	43	.33	83	.12	63
Amount consumed	.32	71	.50	96	.20	57	.38	95	.15	79
Family structure /personality	.45	100	.52	100	.35	100	.40	100	.19	100

B. Women

	Irish r^2	Irish %	Italian r^2	Italian %	Jewish r^2	Jewish %	Swedish r^2	Swedish %	English r^2	English %
Family of origin*	.11	38	.03	13	.08	36	.31	66	.08	27
Present family and friends	.12	41	.06	26	.09	41	.41	81	.19	63
Amount consumed	.25	86	.23	100	.18	82	.46	98	.28	93
Family structure /personality	.29	100	.23	100	.22	100	.47	100	.30	100

* Mother's drinking, father's drinking, family drinking problem, parental approval

Ethnic Drinking Subcultures

CHAPTER SIX
Drug Usage and Drinking Among Ethnic Groups

One of the questions that arise in any consideration of ethnic drinking is whether the different ethnic groups may have different "addiction" subcultures. The Irish, for example, may drink more because they have an "oral dependency" subculture and, hence, are more likely also to smoke cigarettes and, perhaps, marijuana. It is certainly the case (Table 6.1) that the two Catholic groups, which are the most likely to be the heavy drinking groups, are also more likely to smoke cigarettes (about 75 percent of the Catholic adults smoke cigarettes and about two-thirds of the non-Catholics). One out of four Jews reports smoking marijuana, however, and only 17 percent of the Irish and Swedes. There is, perhaps, some evidence of a Catholic "oral dependency" subculture, but it applies only to relatively old-fashioned forms of oral pleasure and not the more recent and more fashionable usage of marijuana. Other NORC research shows that Irish Catholics are second only to Jews in their willingness to approve the legalization of marijuana (1976).

The overwhelming majority of the adolescents of all ethnic groups do not smoke. Interestingly enough, however, young women are more likely to admit to smoking than young men, with one-quarter of the Irish young women and almost one-third of the Italian young women smoking (Table 6.2). Jewish boys are the most likely to have used marijuana (43 percent), and Jewish boys smoke marijuana more often than they smoke cigarettes (16 percent versus 12 percent). There is relatively little difference among English boys in those smoking and those using marijuana often (18 percent versus 17 percent). Italian and Swedish girls are more likely than their male counterparts to say that they use marijuana often (15 percent for Italian girls and 13 percent for Swedish girls, as opposed to 9 percent for both Italian boys and Swedish boys). Italian girls are also the most likely of any of the ethnic groups to say that they have used "pep pills"—though only 13 percent of them so report. It will be remembered that it was Italian young women who also were the most likely to have serious drinking problems, and that the Italian drinking socialization model breaks down among adolescent women.

Putting the use of marijuana and pills together to form a drug-usage scale, we observe in Table 6.3 that, while there are only relatively slight differences in the drug-usage scale among adolescents, Jewish, Italian, and English adolescents are slightly above the mean, and Irish and Swedish adolescents are below the mean. There are, however, very strong correlations between drug usage and drinking problems for all the adolescents.

A simplified version of our adolescent drinking model accounts for two-fifths of the variance in drug usage among adolescents. There is a direct relationship of .40 between alcohol consumption and drug usage among adolescents, and the peer-group drinking environment has a combined direct and indirect influence on drug usage of .50. Those young people who drink a lot and associate with those who also drink a lot are much more likely to use drugs than those who drink less and are in a heavily drinking peer-group environment.

Furthermore, while there is no direct relationship between family affection (as measured by our support factor) and drug usage, support does have an indirect relationship—principally through peer group and liquor consumption—of .28 on drug usage. Even mother's drinking behavior affects drug usage, though again indirectly (.08).

We assume in the model in Figure 6.1 that alcohol consumption precedes drug usage and that both are influenced by the drinking habits of the peer group. Of course, young people influence their peer groups (though hardly as much as they are influenced by them). In the real world, however, it is likely that the influence of the group on the young person's use of alcohol and drugs is likely to be simultaneous rather than sequential, though probably a group begins to experiment with alcohol before it turns to marijuana. However, the drinking behavior of mother and father and the family structure/personality subsystem do affect the kind of peer group in which a young person chooses to associate. The more a young person's parents drink and the less affection there is in the family life, the more a young person is likely to turn to an environment where both drinking and drug usage will occur.

There are conceptual as well as organizational reasons for keeping the various forms of substance abuse distinct. It would appear, however, that for young people they are strongly related and heavily influenced by the peer-group environment; the environment, in turn, is affected by the alcohol usage in the family—but not by the use of either nicotine or marijuana among parents. (There are no significant relationships between parental nicotine and/or marijuana usage and adolescent drug or alcohol usage).

There are also ethnic interactions—different ethnic subcultures—in the relationships between drug usage and alcohol usage (Table 6.4). For the low-drinking and relatively high drug using Jewish culture, the amount of alcohol consumed is a less important predictor of drug usage than is the peer-group drinking behavior. A Jewish young person in a peer group of young people who drink is also more likely to use drugs, regardless of his own drinking, but one's own drinking is a strong predictor of drug usage for the other four groups. Somewhat the reverse is true for the Irish for whom the sheer amount of alcohol consumed is a somewhat stronger predictor of drug usage than the drinking environment. In the light-drinking subculture, the peer-group drinking environment is more important than the amount consumed, while in the heavy-drinking environment, the peer group is less important than it is in other groups.

Mother's drinking behavior is of little importance to the Irish and English but of much greater importance for the other groups (though always through its influence on the drinking environment). Thus, the family-drinking impact on drug usage seems to be limited to three ethnic subcultures, though the impact of family affection—support—is important for all groups. The strength of the relationship between support and drug usage, however, does not vary among the groups.

We note this relationship between our ethnic socialization model and drug usage in passing. We would suggest, however, that further research on adolescent drug use and abuse ought to take both the ethnic factor and alcohol usage into consideration. While the various groups do not differ enormously in their adolescent years in their levels of drug consumption, young people from the different groups seem to find their way into peer-group environments where the propensity to abuse alcohol and drugs is high by somewhat different routes—and to be affected by such environments in somewhat different ways. One can tentatively submit as a subject for further research that there are different substance-abuse subcultures, at least for adolescents.

Figure 6.1

DRINKING AND DRUG USAGE AMONG TEENAGERS

(simplified model)

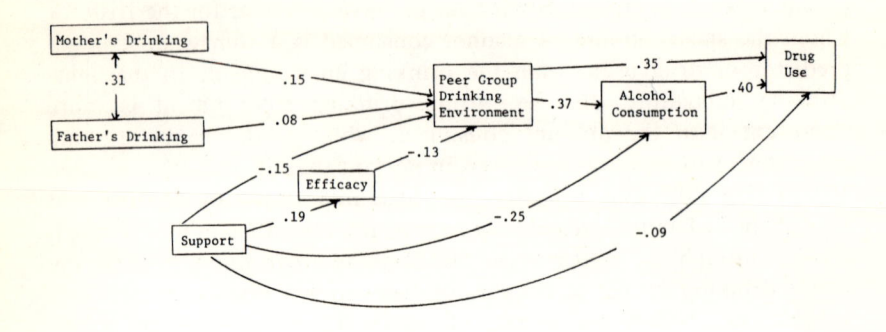

TABLE 6.1

OTHER ADDICTIVE BEHAVIOR IN ETHNIC SUBCULTURES

(Percent)

	Irish	Swedish	Italian	Jewish	English
Cigarettes	77	62	75	66	68
Marijuana	17	13	20	27	14

86   Ethnic Drinking Subcultures

TABLE 6.2

OTHER ADDICTIONS AMONG TEENAGERS BY ETHNIC GROUP

(Percent)

	Smoke Cigarettes	Smoke Marijuana	Smoke Marijuana Often	Pep Pills
Men				
Irish	13	36	11	9
Italian	18	34	9	9
Jewish	12	43	16	7
Swedish	12	27	9	10
English	18	42	17	8
Women				
Irish	26	29	5	8
Italian	30	28	15	13
Jewish	17	33	11	8
Swedish	22	31	13	10
English	20	29	9	10

TABLE 6.3

ADOLESCENT DRUG USAGE SCALE

(Z Scores)

Irish	-.07
Italian	.04
Jewish	.10
Swedish	-.06
English	.04

TABLE 6.4

PRINCIPAL INTERACTIONS WITH ETHNICITY
AND DRUG ABUSE AMONG ADOLESCENTS

	Irish	Italians	Jews	Swedes	English
Total Amount Consumed	.45	.46	.14	.48	.44
Drinking Environment	.38	.47	.45	.45	.53
Mother's Drinking	.05	.19	.24	.16	.05

Drug Usage and Drinking

CHAPTER SEVEN
Drinking Subcultures and Assimilation

With the single exception of the difference between Jewish and Italian adolescent women, our "sleight of hand" exercise in which we make differences disappear, has been successful. We have established the differences of ethnic drinking subcultures—subcultures which are different both in their behavior and in the dynamics of behavior transmission across generational lines—and have explained these differences in terms of socialization experiences; we had to appeal to personality and family structure components of our general model only to explain the differences in drinking problems among adolescents. Ethnic subcultures, in other words, exist because people in different ethnic groups learn different kinds of behaviors in the families in which they grew up, from the spouses they marry, in the environment created by their friends and neighbors and, in the case of the Jews, from their religious heritage. There is nothing mysterious, nothing racist, and certainly nothing chauvinistic about delineating subcultures. While there remain many unexplained aspects of the dynamics of their survival—for example, why is mother's drinking more important than father's in predicting alcohol problems for men in all ethnic groups in both adolescent and adult generations?—ethnicity can easily be perceived, as far as drinking is concerned, at any rate, as a socialization phenomenon.

But will the socialization phenomenon weaken with time? As the immigration experience recedes and self-conscious ethnicity diminishes, will there be a tendency for the different ethnic subcultures to become less distinct? Confident predictions that they will are made by many authors who find the persistence of ethnic subcultures somehow offensive. We attempted to test the durability of ethnic drinking subcultures by the use of five measures of assimilation: educational attainment, number of grandparents born in the United States, closeness of feelings to one's ethnic group, the perceived importance of ethnic background, and neighborhood (Table 7.1).

The more years of education one has the more likely one is to leave behind those ethnic cultural traits that are easily discarded. One would thus expect a positive correlation with alcohol consumption for Jews, a negative correlation for the Irish, a positive correlation with drinking problems for Italians and a negative correlation for Swedes. In fact, however, there are only a few statistically significant correlations for education in Table 7.1. Irish adults do drink less, are less likely to be in a heavy drinking environment, but education has no impact on the drinking problems of adults, and it is precisely the Irish adolescents from better educated Irish families who are more likely to have drinking problems. Similarly, the correlations with drinking for Swedes that are significant run in the opposite of the hypothesized direction.

One would also expect positive correlations for Jews and Italians with the number of grandparents born in the United States and negative correlations for the Irish and the Swedes, since the more likely one's family was to be born in the United States the more likely one is to have discarded specifically ethnic cultural behavior. Irish drinking behavior, however, is totally unaffected by generation. The correlations with alcohol use are in the opposite direction of the one predicted by the assimilationist model for the Swedes, and there are only low correlations with generations for drinking environment and drinking problem for the Italian adolescents (.12). There is, however, substantial positive correlation for Jews between amount consumed annually and number of grandparents born in the United States. The longer a Jewish family has been in the United States the more likely its members are to be heavy drinkers—but not to have greater drinking problems.

If one self-consciously set out to sustain one's own particular ethnic drinking heritage, then it might be expected that there would be positive correlations for the Irish and the Swedes between drinking behavior and closeness to one's own ethnic group and the perceived importance of ethnic background. For the Jews and the Italians the relationships would be negative. There is no correlation at all, however, between closeness to ethnic group and any kind of drinking behavior, and only two significant correlations between the importance of ethnic background and drinking behavior. Only one of these (a .26 for Swedish young people between importance of ethnic background and drinking problems) is in the predicated direction. The −.21 correlation between the importance of being Irish and drinking environment is in the opposite direction. It is precisely those for whom being Irish is important who are somewhat less likely to be in a heavy drinking environment—perhaps because they are more aware of the nature of the Irish drinking subculture.

Finally, if moving out of neighborhoods that are predominantly made up of one's own ethnic group would lead to assimilation within the larger society, which would in turn affect drinking behavior, one would expect negative correlations for Jews and Italians and positive correlations for Irish and Swedes. In fact, there are only statistically significant correlations for Jews. Living in a Jewish neighborhood does correlate negatively with all five dependent variables for Jews. The more likely a Jew is to live in a Jewish neighborhood the less likely he or she is to drink, to be in a heavy drinking environment, and to have a serious drinking problem and the less likely are his or her adolescent children to have serious drinking problems and to be living in heavy drinking environments.

Thus, only one of the five assimilation variables—neighborhood—has a consistent relationship in the predicted direction with the range of drinking behavior variables, and that for only the Jewish ethnic group. Education does lead to a slight decline in Irish drinking and Irish drinking environment scores for adults. Number of generations in the United States leads to a slight increase in adolescent drinking problems for Italians and to a considerable amount of increase in alcohol consumption among Jews. If one looks at the most distinctive aspect of drinking subcultures, the high problem drinking of the Irish and the lack of problem drinking among Jews, none of the assimilation variables affects the Irish in either generation and only living in a non-Jewish neighborhood affects the Jews. The drinking subcultures, then, are remarkably durable. Objective factors like generation, education, or neighborhood do not erode them much, nor do subjective factors like the closeness to ethnic group and importance of ethnic background.*

There remains, of course, the enormously important assimilation impact of ethnic intermarriage. Alba (1976) has observed repeatedly that ethnic intermarriages are increasing. He suggests that this increase signals the end of ethnic subculture. But the suggestion seems to us gratuitous.

Normally, there are not enough ethnic mixed marriages in survey samples to study the impact of exogamy on ethnic subcultural behavior. In the present project, however, there are enough Irish and Jewish mixed marriages to investigate the possibility that such exogamous marriages may erode drinking subcultures (Table 7.2). Exogamous marriages have little impact on the Irish drinking subculture, none at all on adults who enter such marriages, and only 8 standardized points on the problem-drinking scores of the children of such marriages. Indeed, the children of Irish exogamous marriages are even more likely (18 standardized points) to be in heavy drinking environments than Irish offspring of endogamous marriages. If one parent is Irish, in other words, one tends more to be part of the Irish drinking subculture.

The Jewish case is less clear-cut. Marrying outside the Jewish religioethnic community increases the possibility that one will be in a heavy drinking environment and have a drinking problem. The children of such exogamous marriages, however, are no more likely to be in a heavy drinking environment than the children of endogamous Jewish marriages.

*Indeed Irish, Italian and Jewish adolescents in the present study are *more* likely than their parents to say that they are close to their ethnic group and that ethnicity is important to them.

There is, nonetheless, some difference (15 standardized points) between the children of exogamous Jewish marriages and the children of endogamous marriages. Interestingly enough, the differences are much more striking among Jews for adults entering the exogamous marriage than for the children who are the products of such unions. Thus, if one of one's parents is Irish, one is Irish as far as one's drinking behavior is concerned; and if one of the parents is Jewish, one is very likely also to be Jewish in drinking behavior—though there will be a bit more difference between these persons and the products of endogamous Jewish marriages than there would be for comparable Irish Catholics.

Drinking subcultures, then, survive not only such assimilation influences such as education, movement out of ethnic neighborhoods, generation in the United States, and decline of ethnic self-consciousness, they also survive ethnic exogamy.

The dynamics of such survival are beyond explanation to be derived by us from the present data. This is obviously a fascinating and important challenge. But the question of the survival of ethnic subcultural characteristics after exogamous marriage is something to be studied and not to be either facilely assumed or denied.

TABLE 7.1

"ASSIMILATION" VARIABLES AND DRINKING BEHAVIOR BY ETHNIC GROUP

(Only Statistically Significant "r's" Are Shown)

	Adults			Adolescents	
	Total oz./year	Environment	Problem	Environment	Problem
EDUCATION					
Irish	-.10	-.17	--	--	.13
Italian	--	--	--	--	--
Jewish	--	--	--	--	--
Swedish	--	.24	.22	--	--
NUMBER OF GRANDPARENTS BORN IN U.S.					
Irish	--	--	--	--	--
Italian	--	--	--	.12	.12
Jewish	.28	--	--	--	--
Swedish	.19	.12	--	--	--
HOW CLOSE ONE FEELS TO ETHNIC GROUP					
Irish	--	--	--	--	--
Italian	--	--	--	--	--
Jewish	--	--	--	--	--
Swedish	--	--	--	--	--
PROPORTION OF NEIGHBORHOOD OWN ETHNIC GROUP					
Irish	--	--	--	--	--
Italian	--	--	--	--	--
Jewish	-.17	-.14	-.36	-.17	-.14
Swedish	--	--	--	--	--
IMPORTANCE OF ETHNIC BACKGROUND					
Irish	--	-.21	--	--	--
Italian	--	--	--	--	--
Jewish	--	--	--	--	--
Swedish	--	--	--	--	.26

TABLE 7.2

DRINKING AND ETHNIC INTERMARRIAGE

(Z Scores)*

	Irish		Jews	
	Endogamous	Exogamous	Endogamous	Exogamous
Adult				
Environment	.03	−.01	−.13	.31
Problem	.00	.00	−.07	.27
Adolescent				
Environment	−.11	.07	.00	.01
Problem	.04	−.04	−.04	.12
N =	(175)	(102)	(30)	(102)

*Z Scores are based on the mean and standard deviation of each ethnic group, not the whole sample.

CHAPTER EIGHT
Conclusion

By way of brief summary, we have established the following points:

1. There are different drinking subcultures among the ethnic groups studied. These subcultures influence the drinking behavior of the friends one chooses, one's own personal drinking behavior, and one's propensity to have drinking problems. Such subcultures generally follow the patterns first described in the ethnic drinking literature of 20 years ago.

2. These subcultures are remarkably durable, persisting across three generations. Although they are less clearly delineated among adolescents, perhaps because of the enormous influence of peer group, there are substantial signs that as peer-group influence wanes the subcultures will strongly reassert themselves among the adolescents as they grow older—especially in the critical area of problem drinking (Chapter 3).

3. A general "socialization" model, together with a consideration of Jewish religiousness can account for most of the differences both in alcohol consumption and problem drinking in both generations and in both sexes among the various ethnic groups. In some cases, these models explain approximately half the variance in drinking behavior (Chapter 4).

4. The socialization model varies considerably among ethnic groups. Thus, there are ethnic subcultures not merely in the drinking outcomes but in the relative strength of the various socialization inputs—our family structural variables are important for some groups and not for others in leading to drinking problems; the influence of spouse and father and mother also vary greatly from group to group (Chapter 5).

5. While the state of the art on the subject of ethnic family diversity permits only speculation as to the reasons for the variety of socialization mechanisms summarized in point 4 (save for Irish men, for whom a substantial theoretical literature exists), the differences are of such a magnitude and such importance that those members of the helping professions who deal with drinking problems can ill afford to be unacquainted with them (Chapter 5).

6. None of the subcultural differences seem to be eroding, either through such "assimilating" forces as importance of ethnic group, education, and generation, or through the proportion of one's ethnic group in one's neighborhood (save for some erosion in the Jewish drinking culture from living in non-Jewish neighborhoods). There are also parallels

in the socialization dynamics across generational lines, especially in the importance of maternal drinking (Chapter 7).

The two major innovations brought to this project have been the use of a socialization model and the application of an ethnic-group perspective, the former developed from a search for an explanation for the differences uncovered by the latter. A discovery made in the course of the project—that drinking socialization processes are different for men and women—might be considered a third innovation. The finding of a linkage between drug usage and alcohol usage among teenagers *in a socialization mechanism,* if not exactly an innovation, is at least a useful insight.

The importance of a mixture of the three innovations to research on alcoholism is briefly sketched in Table 8.1. Every one of the variables from our original drinking-socialization model has an impact on a drinking problem for *someone,* but only one of them—the drinking environment of one's friends—has an impact on everyone's drinking problems (and even the importance of this influence varies greatly between ethnic groups and between the sexes). For all the other variables, if one is asked whether it affects problem drinking, one must respond by saying that it depends on age, sex, and ethnic group, and any answer that ignores one of these three factors is bound to be inaccurate—hence our insistence on the extraordinary importance of our findings for the helping professions. We candidly believe that it would be most unwise to refer a problem drinker to a helping professional who was not sensitive to the kind of diversity we have reported. One cannot, for example, treat an Irish alcoholic like a Jewish alcoholic or an Italian alcoholic, and one cannot even treat an Irish woman alcoholic like an Irish man alcoholic; to do so risks making tragic mistakes in understanding the dynamics of the person's problem.

Our approach to this project began with an ethnic perspective and a conviction that the application of this perspective to alcohol research would be beneficial to both the understanding of drinking behavior and the understanding of American ethnic diversity. The marriage between the two interests seems to have borne enough fruit for us to suggest the three following continuations:

1. The only reason for choosing the groups studied was that a research tradition about their drinking behavior exists. Anecdotally, one hears of other drinking subcultures—Polish, Slovene, Hispanic, native American, Asian American. There is also some evidence, mentioned in passing in the present work, that there also exists a Baptist Methodist nondrinking culture not unlike that of the Jews. If the variety described in this book exists among the five ethnic groups studied, it would certainly seem to be appropriate to explore the possible existence of other drinking subcultures. It would be bad science and risky policy to exclude on a priori grounds the

possibility of such other diversity in drinking behavior.

2. At a later time, it would be useful to return to the adolescents studied in the present project to see how the drinking socialization model may change as they grow older and as the peer group influence begins to wane.

3. While we can rather successfully account for the differences in drinking outcome, we are reduced mostly to speculation as to the reasons for the differences in the dynamics of drinking socialization among the groups. Why, for example, is mother's drinking unimportant for the Irish and important for other groups? Why is father's drinking and his serious drinking problem antecedent of a serious drinking problem for an Irish adult woman and for no one else? We must know a good deal more than we do now about the dynamics of family relationships in the various ethnic communities if we are going to arrive at explanations. Such anaysis, we would submit, would require a close cooperation between survey work and sophisticated field observation.

This third recommendation provides an opportunity for us to say something about the concept of ethnic subculture. In any society, particularly one as large as the United States, human attitudes and behaviors vary greatly around the mean. A subculture is nothing more than a group of people, connected by some common experience, whose variations tend to be of a certain magnitude and a certain direction. These variations may represent a deviation from the "common culture" (by which, presumably, is meant the mean), but they are not in isolation from it. Thus, none of the variations in drinking problems went as much as a single standard deviation above or below the mean. There are, in other words, some Irish men who do not drink at all and some Jewish men who drink heavily. A subculture, then, is a group whose mean and standard deviation on a given measure are somewhat above or below those of others. It is difficult to see how a society can avoid having subcultures when they are so defined.

Such group variations from the national mean may be the result of geography, others may result from race, sex, and the complex of things we call "ethnicity"; that is to say, the common experience that leads to a subcultural variation may come from many causes. However, once one has established such a subcultural variation linked to a specific common experience, one is then faced with the challenge of explaining its origins: one must ask what there is in the common experience of a specific group that leads it to a variation from the national mean score.

In this book we have asked such a question on the specific issue of variety of drinking behavior, and we have asked it of those subcultures whose common experience is related to religioethnic background. What is it, in other words, in the common experience of Jews, as opposed to Irish, that makes them less likely—on the average—to drink.

We have suggested that much of the explanation can be found by looking at one's subtle interactions with one's parents, spouses, friends, both in the direction imitation of their behavior and in the use of power and affection in that relationship. We assumed that an extraordinary variety of complex influences shape the behavior patterns of adult men and women, that many of these influences are subtle and generally unperceived both by those influencing and being influenced, and that it is likely to be shaped by the template of what is appropriate behavior that religioethnic groups bring to family life for a son or for a daughter. Precisely because they are both subtle and unperceived, these patterns of expectations and interactions are internalized early and rather completely and transmitted to the next generation quite un-self-consciously.

What is the common experience of those of, let us say, Irish Catholic background that leads them to vary from the national problem-drinking mean? We would suggest that it is the common experience of being raised Irish Catholic—in the sense that the interactions and expectations in *some* Irish Catholic families have a propensity to lead to higher levels of alcohol consumption (than in many Jewish families, by way of comparison) and greater tendencies toward alcohol problems.

That is our conception of what a subculture is—different mean scores and different common experiences (which of course mean different mean scores on the experience measures and not totally different experiences)—that and nothing more.

We would submit that our use of this conception of subculture has proved useful in exploring drinking behavior and that there is, then, reason to assume that it might be useful in exploring other behavior, and three concluding comments are therefore in order.

First, if such critics of "ethnic chauvinism" as Orlando Patterson are to be taken seriously, one ought not even examine the persistence of such ethnic diversity as has been described here. Leaving aside the curious irony of a universalism that outlaws certain areas of scholarly research, we still must observe that, if information about the varieties of ethnic drinking subcultures are denied them, alcohol counselors, clinicians, and educators, and policy makers will be seriously impeded in their work.

Second, one is hard put to determine how the variety of ethnic drinking subcultures described in this book are a threat either to the American common culture or to universalist principals, as Patterson would seem to suggest. It is a misfortune, perhaps, that the Irish drink as much as they do, and are so prone to alcohol problems. One could easily urge moderation or abstinence on them in terms of physical or psychological health, but it is somewhat bizarre to suggest that they are chauvinist, fascist, or reactionary because they drink more than other people. Similarly, if the elimination of ethnic subcultural diversity is desirable to preserve the universalistic world view and the common culture, then one will have to insist just as vigorously that Jews drink more and acquire more serious drinking problems. Such a reductio ad absurdum seems to suggest that Patterson's conceptual framework (1978) is severely limited.

Instead of conceptualizing subcultures as standing in opposition to the general, common, or universalistic culture, one might more usefully conceptualize them as additions to the general culture. It is lamentable that the Irish drink as much as they do, but this drinking does not interfere with their general political liberalism, their considerable economic success, their high level of educational attainment, their commitment to racial integration (highest of any Gentile group in the United States), or their commitment to civil liberties (again the highest of any Gentile group). Doubtless some forms of subcultural deviation could conceivably interfere with the universalist values or commitment to the common cultural vision; but the existence and impact of such deviant and divisive subcultural behaviors ought to be demonstrated and investigated and not simply assumed.

Third, it may be well demonstrated by this study that there are durable ethnic drinking subcultures that can be accounted for by socialization models and that show no signs of being "assimilated" out of existence; but it then could be said that that doesn't prove there are other subcultural varieties of behavior that also persist. We are prepared to concede the point, though differences in religion (McCready 1976) and political participation (Greely 1974, 1975) have already been demonstrated. But whether there are other ethnic subcultural behaviors parallel to the drinking subcultures is a matter for empirical investigation and not for a priori assumption—at least as long as sociology remains an empirical discipline.

TABLE 8.1

PROBLEM DRINKING AND PREDICTOR VARIABLES

Father's drinking	Only Irish women
Mother's drinking	Italian, English and Swedish men; Italian and Jewish boys; Jewish, Swedish and English girls
Parental approval	Negative for all men except Swedish, positive for Swedes
Drinking problem	Irish and Swedish women
Spouse	Swedish men, negative for Jewish men
Friends	All
Power	Adult women, Swedish boys
Support	Girls, Irish men
Efficacy	Irish and Jewish men

APPENDIX A
Data Collection Methodology

The data for the study were obtained as part of a NORC survey conducted between April and August 1978 on family life in the United States. The research was funded by a grant from the Department of Health, Education and Welfare (Grant #AA 02k22-02). The sampling requirements posed by the theoretical assumptions of the survey that pertain to ethnic patterns of family socialization and the intergenerational transmission of values presented an unusual number of problems not normally encountered in national random-sample survey efforts. Since the focus of the study was on five distinct ethnic groups, each of which represents only a small percent of the national population, a cost analysis of the random-sampling process established that enormous interviewer expenses would be incurred in filling the quota of two hundred individuals for each of the ethnic groups.

Census statistics indicated that individuals belonging to the five groups composing the sample lived predominately in urban areas in the eastern and midwestern regions of the United States. The decision was made to sacrifice the generalizability of a *national* random sample for the convenience and savings of a random sample of the five ethnic populations within four major cities. The ethnic concentration of Jews and Irish in New York and Chicago was a primary determinant in targeting these two major cities in the survey. In addition, the concentration of Irish and Italians in Boston was the basis for its inclusion.

From the onset of the project, it was recognized that of the five ethnic groups, the members of the Swedish community would be the most difficult to identify because of their relatively small numbers in the total population and their non-nucleated immigration settlement patterns. Since the Minneapolis-St. Paul area has one of the highest statistical proportions of Swedish Americans in the country, the Twin Cities were included as the fourth site for the survey. Estimates of the ethnic distribution in each of the sample cities were obtained from the figures generated by NORC's General Social Survey of the American Population for 1972 to 1976 (Table A.1).

Because of the low selection ratio stemming from the strict screening requirements of the sample as well as the high cost of household interviewing, it was decided that the most efficient way of identifying the sample respondents was through the use of random-digit dialing. Following this procedure a list of sample phone numbers was generated for each of the four metropolitan areas included in the study. Creating the phone numbers involved a two-step process. First, a list of all the three-digit telephone exchanges in each of the cities was obtained. Second, from a stored table of random numbers, a computer generated a series of four digits to go with the exchange numbers. The result was a random set of possible working phone numbers for each area. Table A.2 contains the total numbers generated and the dispositions recorded for the total sample by city.

As expected, a high proportion of numbers (39.7%) was not in use by the phone company during the time of the survey, and a considerable number were being used for business purposes (18.9%). Only phones located in domestic dwelling units were eligible for inclusion in the final sample.

The selection of the final sample was compounded in difficulty by the fact that there were two criteria for selection. The first, as noted, was that parent respondents had to identify either ethnic background or that of their spouses as one of the five included in the study and, second, the individual also had to be the parent of an adolescent child between the ages of twelve and seventeen. Sampling estimates of households with adolescent children were obtained from census figures and Internal Revenue Service sources. Since no explicit data were available for individual ethnic groups and the number of operating telephone numbers in each city could only be estimated, an initial sampling frame of numbers was only an educated guess of how many numbers would be needed to produce the requisite number of cases.

In the event that more than one adult or adolescent in a household met the eligibility requirements, the telephone interviewer was instructed to choose the sample participant according to the individual designated on a miniature Kish table attached to the screening label.* The table was constructed to provide an even distribution of males and females and to insure a full range of ages among the adolescents.

Following the identification of the sample respondents, questionnaires were sent to each participating family with directions, parental permission forms granting approval for their adolescent to participate in the study, a short flyer about NORC and its research interests, and two two-dollar bills as an expression of the organization's appreciation for the respondent's time and effort (See Appendix B). The cash incentive had two advantages over an institutionally signed check or

*A Kish table, for example, tells the interviewer that if there are four eligble respondents in this dwelling unit, they should select the second. These selections are determined probabilistically and they change from case to case.

voucher. First, since the two-dollar bill is still a novelty in many households, it was expected to have more of an impact and perhaps elicit from recipients more of a commitment to complete the questionnaire than other forms of payment. Second, since two questionnaires were sent to each household, the two bills facilitated splitting the incentive between the parent and adolescent. Previous survey research using cash incentives indicated that a plateau effect exists in the response rates generated by increasing the monetary reward for participation in surveys (see Wotrube 1966). Although three dollars has been shown to be the threshhold beyond which incremental changes in the incentives produced little increase in return rates, it was decided that the rate of inflation over the past four or five years, coupled with the convenience and appeal of the double two-dollar-bill incentive warranted raising the cash inducement to four dollars.

Self-administered questionnaire surveys are generally beset by two methodological problems. First, response rates are usually considerably lower than those obtained in interviewer-administered questions. Second, in a random sample of the population that is not screened in any way there is no way of ascertaining possible nonresponse biases in the population. Since inclusion in the sample was highly specified by ethnicity and offspring, we already knew something about the respondents before the mailing. At the time of the screener, additional information including name, and religious background was also obtained from each respondent contacted unless the screener was refused. Table A.3 gives the figures for the number of respondents who ultimately refused the questionnaire.

At the end of the pretest, each respondent was asked whether he or she would have answered the same questions had they been asked in person by an interviewer. Of the 64 pretest respondents, 52 percent said that they would have not answered the questions or would have much preferred answering them privately in a self-administered format. The respondents also indicated that the truthfulness of their answers might have been adversely affected had the personal-interview structure been adopted. In the study itself, 67 percent of the respondents indicated that they would not have answered the questions in a face-to-face administration of the questionnaire.

As noted earlier, low response rates are a troublesome part of self-administered survey questionnaires. While professional survey-research organizations rarely settle for completion rates of less than 80 percent on interviewer-administered surveys, the acceptable response mean is considerably lower for mailed surveys. One of the better introductory survey research methodology books notes that "a response rate of at least 50% is *adequate* for analysis and reporting. A response rate of at least 60% is *good*. And a response rate of 70% is *very* good (Babbie 1973: 165; emphasis on original).

Despite the fact that the response rates in the present survey were expected to be adversely affected as a result of the sensitive nature of some of the questions that touched on areas such as drinking and family relationships, high quality and quantity response standards were set for the survey. It was decided from the outset that a 70 percent return rate would be a minimum goal of the project. A final completed return rate in excess of 80% was viewed as excellent. In anticipation that up to 30 percent of the accepted respondents would not complete the questionnaire, a short refusal instrument was developed in order to obtain a few demographic and behavioral pieces of information in order to determine the extent of possible sample bias.

Whenever possible, questions about the primary dependent variables were made compatible with questions used in previous studies in order to facilitate longitudinal and cohort comparisons. In a number of instances, wordings were changed slightly to improve readability and clarity.

The importance of interviewer rapport with the respondent has been noted frequently in survey research (Human 1954: Williams 1959). This study posed particular problems in this regard since the only direct contact the respondent may have had with the project personnel was in the initial telephone call at the time of the screening. As a result, particular emphasis was placed on the manner and delivery of the telephone interviewers. Each interviewer was trained by the NORC staff during five-hour sessions given on consecutive days. During this period considerable attention was paid to enhancing the smoothness of the interviewer's delivery—a process complicated by the complexity of the screener, which required a substantial amount of information to be hand recorded. In additiion, one complete training session was spent taping mock interviews followed by playback and critique sessions. At the culmination of the training program each of the interviewers made calls to unidentified NORC personnel familiar with the goals of the survey. The role-playing episode of the training process not only enhanced the delivery of the interviewers; it also prepared them to handle most of the respondent questions and awkward situations that could be anticipated during the course of the study.

While the actual fieldwork was being carried out, daily counts were kept of the number of calls made by each member of the interviewing staff as well as the number of refusals and abrupt terminations of the telephone conservations. The figures presented in Table A.4 are for those completed calls made during a seven-hour working day between the hours of 2 p.m. and 9 p.m.

Because of the sensitive nature of some of the questions in the survey as well as the restrictions placed on the type of information that can be gathered in survey research within the guidelines laid down by the Elementary and Secondary Education Act of 1965 (Title V, Section 513 amendments) the NORC advisory board and legal staff felt that the interest of the organization and the respondents would be best served by requiring that a parental release form be sent to all participating families. Consent for the child's participation had to be obtained in order for the data to be included in the analysis. Since confidentiality of responses was extremely important for a number of adolescents, especially those admitting to various forms of deviant behavior, each adolescent could return his or her questionnaire in a separate envelope. In the first one-third of the Chicago sample, 15 percent of the adult respondents were given the option of removing the cover page of the questionnaire which had their names written on it and making instead some some sort of identifying mark on both their questionnaires and their children's for matching purposes. This procedure guaranteed complete anonymity to the respondent while at the same time enabling the NORC staff to match parent and adolescent questionnaires. None of the families availed themselves of this opportunity so the procedure was dropped for the remainder of the study. It would appear that respondents either accept the survey institution's promise of confidentiality or they do not. If the latter is the case, there are few guarantees that can induce the respondent to participate.

Experience with the pretest responses corroborated the literature on the negative effects of time lapse on response rates (Bailey 1978: Ch. 7). The pretest returns indicated that if the questionnaires were not returned within 10 to 14 days from the time of mailing, the probability of their being returned at all fell dramatically. Consequently, survey packets were sent to the selected respondents immediately after the individuals were accepted. In the letter accompanying the materials, respondents were urged to complete and return the survey instrument within two days of receipt. Although six days was the minimum amount of time possible to receive a completed questionnaire from the time it was sent out, 60 percent of the final returns came back within ten days.

On the sixth day after the mailing, each respondent for whom we had not received a returned packet was called on the phone and asked if their copy of the survey had been delivered and if they had any questions about the instrument or procedures. The call served as a reminder and an opportunity to reassure vacillating respondents and also as a check on the reliability of the postal system.

If the completed questionnaire was not received in the following week, a reminder flyer was sent to each family soliciting their cooperation. If another full week passed without any communications from the respondent, he or she was called again with the intent of administering the refusal questionnaire. At this time the caller, a member of the NORC supervisory staff, pursued any sign of the person's willingness to complete the questionnaire. Individuals who refused at this stage were asked to answer a few questions about their reasons for not completing the instrument as well as several questions that enabled us to weigh the sample to account for nonrespondent bias. Individuals who still said that they would complete the questionnaire were given another week to return their packets after which they were called back a third time and asked to complete the refusal instrument (See Appendix C).

Potential respondents who refused the initial screener even before it was determined whether they were eligible to participate in the survey were telephoned again in an attempt to gain a satisfactory disposition of their eligibility. Although many of these individuals again refused to participate, dispositions were obtained for all but 3 percent of our 20,000 cases. It is obvious that persistent efforts of the interview staff paid off, not only in terms of reducing the number of "no dispositions," but in increasing the number of respondents who were eventually accepted. The final mean response rate obtained by dividing the number of "complete family" returned questionnaires by the number of families mailed questionnaires was 89 percent. The variation in response rates by city and ethnicity was given in Table 4.5

The absolute response rate also takes into account the individuals who were screened into the sample but refused to participate in the survey. The absolute rate is calculated by dividing the percent of the sample who agreed to participate by those who were accepted and multiplying the quotient by the return rate.

$$\text{Absolute response rate} = \frac{\text{No. of questionnaires mailed} \times \text{response rate}}{\text{No. of families accepted}}$$

$$= \frac{1,107}{1,265} \times .89$$

$$= 78\%$$

Given the difficulty of eliciting the separate cooperation of two individuals from each family and considering the complexity of the questionnaire, an absolute response rate of this magnitude speaks well for the representatives of the final sample to the sample population as a whole.

TABLE A-1

ESTIMATED ETHNIC COMPOSITION OF SAMPLE CITIES BASED ON THE GENERAL
SOCIAL SURVEY OF THE AMERICAN POPULATION, 1972-1976

		BOSTON	NEW YORK	CHICAGO	MINN-ST. PAUL
Irish	A	.06	.08	.06	.10
	B	.16	.04	.11	.05
	C	.11	.05	.09	.07
Italian	A	.23	.18	.04	.16
	B	.27	.18	.04	.00
	C	.25	.18	.04	.07
British	A	.03	.03	.05	.06
	B	.11	.02	.05	.11
	C	.07	.03	.05	.09
Scandinavian	A	.03	.03	.00	.16
	B	.00	.01	.04	.23
	C	.01	.02	.03	.19
Jew	A	.09	.28	.11	.00
	B	.05	.10	.06	.14
	C	.07	.17	.08	.07
Total proportion of pop. accounted for by these ethnic groups.	A	.44	.60	.26	.48
	B	.59	.35	.30	.53
	C	.51	.45	.29	.49

A = 1972-1973 GSS's
B = 1974, 1975 and 1976 GSS's
C = 1972 through 1976 GSS's

TABLE A-2

DISPOSITION OF RANDOMLY GENERATED
TELEPHONE NUMBERS IN SAMPLE

	Chicago	Minn.	New York	Boston	Total
Number of generated phone numbers	19,795	15,606	7,379	7,649	50,429
Number of vacant lines	7,845	6,606	2,331	3,279	20,061
Number of business lines	3,394	3,017	1,750	1,395	9,556
Net Sample	8,556	5,983	3,298	2,975	20,813

Table A-3: Refusal Rate and Nature of Refusals

Refusal Rate

	Irish	Italian	Jewish	Swedish	English
Number of Families Screened into Sample	326	228	149	176	228
Number of Families that Refused or Did Not Return Questionnaire	42	38	15	14	16
Percent refusals	13%	17%	10%	8%	7%
Net Sample	284	190	134	162	212

Nature of Refusals

Refusals where no reason was given	91
Refusals where reason was given	34
Total	125

Reason for refusal when given (N = 34)

Could not find time	11	32%
Questions were too personal	7	20%
Forgot to mail it or lost it, etc.	7	20%
Did not think this was appropriate for my child	6	18%
It was too long	3	9%

108   Appendix A

TABLE A-4

NATURE OF FINAL DISPOSITIONS DURING
SCREENING PHASE OF SURVEYS BY CITY.

	Chicago	Minneapolis	New York	Boston
Number of Screened In Respondents	405	353	185	323
Number of Respondents Screened Out	7,744	5,413	2,900	2,497
Respondent Initially Refused to Talk or Broke Off Conversation	55	81	--	35
Final Refusals After Conversion Attempt	263	133	125	103
Respondent Spoke No English, Was Too Ill to Participate, etc.	89	3	88	17
Net Sample	8,556	5,983	3,298	2,975

TABLE A-5

RESPONSE RATES BY CITY AND ETHNICITY

Total			Irish	Italian	Jewish	Swedish	English
327 92.4%	Chicago	N %	95 92.2%	73 90.1%	54 94.7%	35 89.7%	70 94.6%
292 93.4%	Minneapolis	N %	61 87.1%	11 100.0%	15 93.8%	121 93.8%	84 96.6%
123 78.9%	New York	N %	26 81.2%	48 73.8%	45 84.9%	-- --	4 57.1%
238 83.9%	Boston	N %	102 84.3%	58 80.5%	20 86.9%	6 75.0%	52 86.7%
980 88.9%	Total Total	N %	284 87.3%	190 83.6%	134 90.1%	162 92.2%	210 92.7%

APPENDIX B
Comparison of Respondents and Non-respondents: The Refused Interview

From the outset of the research project the survey team was aware of the difficulty of obtaining high response rates due to both the sensitive nature of the questions and the difficulty in securing questionnaires from both a parent and an adolescent in each family. In order to estimate the confounding effects of response bias a refusal questionnaire was drawn up and administered to all eligible respondents who refused to participate in the survey.

As noted in Appendix A, a total of 1260 families were screened into the sample. Of that number, a total of 1102 families agreed to receive the questionnaire. The survey staff was able to administer the 13-question refusal questionnaire to 80 adult respondents. Thus, 28.3% of the eligible families who refused to accept or complete the original questionnaire did agree to complete the refusal questionnaire. The 80 refusal respondents represent 64.5% of the total number of families who were mailed questionnaires but did not return them.

The principal reasons for refusing to complete the original questionnaire fall into two general categories. As can be seen in Table B.1, the majority of the respondents replied that they refused to complete the questionnaire because either the questions were too personal or because they felt that they did not have enough time to answer them. When the responses are grouped by categories, 48.6% of the respondents indicate that they did not have the time to participate or that they were just not interested in the project; the same proportion also replied that they did not like surveys or did not trust assurances of confidentiality. Nearly 19% of the respondents refused for reasons including deaths in the family and hospitalization.

One of the concerns of the research staff was that potential respondents with higher levels of education might be more reluctant to complete the questionnaire than those with lower levels of education since the former might be more reluctant to answer sensitive questions concerning income, occupational satisfaction, and drinking behavior. As

Table B.2 indicates, however, respondents with less than a high school education were more likely *not* to complete the original questionnaire than respondents with more than high school training.

Assuming that there was a random distribution of the population among those individuals who only accepted the refusal questionnaire and those who completed the original questionnaire, it appears that the more education a person has, the more likely he or she was to complete the survey questionnaire. It is possible, however, that the individuals who refused to participate in the survey also rejected the refusal questionnaire. If this interpretation is correct, it indicates that the better-educated respondents who refused the survey questionnaire tended to reject the refusal questionnaire as well. No substantial differences exist between the two columns, indicating that there is not a substantial educational bias in the sample.

It is important to recall that a family was not included in the final sample unless both the adult and the adolescent returned their respective questionnaires. The figures in Table B.3 reveal that a family that contains an adolescent child whose grades are reported as *excellent*—that is, mostly A's and B's—was much more likely to complete the survey questionnaire than a family with a child who is only an average student. Again assuming a random distribution of grades among those students who completed the questionnaire and those who accepted only the refusal questionnaire, it is striking that 18.3% more students participated in the survey who got A's and B's in school. On the other hand, 39.8% more of the families with students reporting mostly C's for grades completed the refusal questionnaire than agreed to participate.

Unfortunately, it is impossible for us to delineate which of two reasons accounts for these differences. First, it could be that students coming from homes that stress responsibility and whose parents are highly educated and highly motivated are more likely to complete the questionnaire because of favorable environmental encouragement. The second possibility is that students who have low levels of motivation, manifested by low grades independent of home background, are simply less disposed to participating in projects of this sort. Another possible explanation of the response difference is that families with good students may be refusing to complete *both* the survey questionnaire and the refusal questionnaire.

One of the important variables in this study was the support dimension of family structure. One of the key variables in this factor measured happiness within the household. As can be seen in Table B.4, there were no significant differences between the respondents in the first two categories. A notable discrepancy, however, does occur among the "not too happy"; 16.1% of the survey respondents answered "not too happy" as opposed to only 5.3% of the refusing respondents. The literature on response patterns in survey data indicates that a psychological set was perhaps produced in the respondents answering the survey questions. In other words, it may be that answering a series of questions on family life caused the respondents to recall more accurately the quality of their home environments. Since the refusal questionnaire was administered over the telephone and because the respondent encountered this question suddenly and out of context with other questions about home family life, it may very well be that the respondent was not able to reflect on the question as carefully as the individuals who had a self-administered instrument. The result is that the respondent is more likely to give a "happy" response than a "not too happy" one.

Another of the questions used in calculating the support dimension ascertained how close the respondent was to his or her father or step-father. Table B.5 shows that there are some differences between the respondents although not substantial ones; 8.5% more refusal respondents said that they were close to their fathers. At the same time, 9.4% more individuals who participated in the survey said that they were not. This response pattern is similar to the one found in Table B.4. Again, it seems likely that the differences result primarily from a response set. Although there is very little divergence between the percentages of those responding "pretty close," it is most likely that the respondents who completed the questionnaire adjusted their opinion of their relationship with their fathers or step-fathers downward from the first row to the second and from the second row to the third row as they answered the questions.

There were small differences between the refusing respondents and the questionnaire respondents in terms of their fathers' approving or disapproving of people having drinks containing alcohol when they were 16 (Table B.6). Approximately 10% more of the individuals of those refusing responded that their fathers disapproved of serving drinks. This is in line with an overall conservative bias evidenced by the refusal respondents as will be seen more clearly in subsequent tables.

The median age of all respondents was 40-49 (Table B.7). There were negligible differences between any of the age categories indicating that no age bias exists in the final sample.

The slightly more conservative bias evident in the respondents who completed the refusal questionnaire appears in Tables B.8 and B.9. Although the differences between the two types of respondents are small in both tables, it is apparent that 5.3% *fewer* survey respondents said that they currently serve drinks to guests in their home (Table B.8). Similarly, in Table B.9 6.4% fewer survey participants said that they currently drink alcoholic beverages. Although this gives credence to the more conservative bias of the refusal respondents, the differences do not indicate a significant bias in the sample of respondents who completed the questionnaire.

Table B.10 also sustains the more conservative nature of the respondents completing the refusal questionnaire as almost 16% more refusal respondents classify themselves as infrequent drinkers. The percentage differences for those classifying themselves as moderate drinkers and those who drink quite a bit are virtually insignificant. There exists again, however, the possibility of a psychological response set at work here. Individuals who completed the original questionnaire were exposed to a considerable number of questions dealing with drinking. Thus, when they encountered a self-rate question of this sort, they were likely to be less inhibited in giving a truthful response. A respondent who was asked this question over the telephone did not find the question embedded in a series of drinking questions as did the person who completed the self-administered questionnaire. Therefore, there is the possibility that the 16% may be accounted for not only by the more conservative nature of the respondent but also by the situational nature of the question.

As to the question of how much the individual respondent would miss drinking if he or she had to give it up all together, some substantial differences emerged as can be see in Table B.11. Over 10% more of the respondents who completed the questionnaire said that they would miss drinking somewhat. On the other hand, 66% of those completing the refusal questionnaire said that they would not miss drinking at all versus only 43% of those who completed the questionnaire. This is a total difference of over 22%. It seems unlikely that a psychological response set could account for a difference this large, especially for the "not at all" category. It is probable that substantive dissimilarities do exist among the respondents on this issue.

As a final control for differences in drinking behavior we asked the refusal respondents what type of help or advice they would seek if there were a drinking problem in their family. Table B.12 shows the differences between the refusal respondents and those who completed the survey questionnaire. Unfortunately, the two questionnaires are not directly comparable. In the survey the respondent was able to reply to either of the first two categories; that is, he or she could have answered that the problem would be solved within the family as well as with outside help. In the refusal questionnaire, the respondent was asked to reply to one of three choices. The survey respondent only had 2 choices. Therefore, the difference of 13% in the response in the "solve in family" row are most likely accounted for by the 17% who answered "both" in the refusal column. The incompatibility of the question makes direct comparisons of the two columns suspect.

A comparison of the occupational status of the refusal respondents and the questionnaire respondents indicates that there were no substantial differences between the two samples (Table B.13). Nearly 55% of the respondents in both categories are working full time. In the second major occupational status category, those who are working part-time, there is only a 5.5 percent difference between the refusal and survey respondents.

In the third principal category, housekeepers, there is only a 4% difference between the respondents. We conclude that, with regard to education and occupational status, the sample used in the analysis contains no substantial bias relating to background characteristics.

To summarize the findings of the refusal questionnaire, it appears that no substantial discrepancies exist within our sample of final respondents. Of course, we have no way of estimating the nature of the responses for those individuals who refused to complete even a refusal questionnaire. However, on the basis of the findings we were able to obtain from the 80 respondents who refused to complete the survey questionnaire, it would appear that our unmeasured are likely to be even more conservative than any of the individuals in our sample and they are likely to have, or at least admit to, fewer drinking problems. It is possible for some of our critics to argue that our findings with regard to problem drinking and the behavioral and attitudinal manifestations of those problems are overly pessimistic. To answer that charge, we can only reply that while this may be true it is equally plausible that respondents with the most egregious drinking problems are also very likely to be unwilling to respond to questions concerning drinking and related forms of behavior. Response biases are endemic to social-survey research and especially to research involving controversial and sensitive topics such as drinking. We have taken all the precautionary measures feasible to prevent such a bias emerging from our final sample, and on the basis of our refusal interviews we are confident that the distributional nature of our findings approximates very closely the entire population of eligible respondents.

TABLE B-1

REASON FOR REFUSAL: WOULD YOU TELL ME WHY YOU DECIDED NOT TO COMPLETE YOUR QUESTIONNAIRE?

Questionnaire too long	8.7 %
Not enough time	29.9
Questions too personal	23.7
Don't like surveys in general	9.9
Don't trust assurance of confidentiality	12.5
Don't like questions about drinking	0.0
Don't want my child answering questions like these	2.5
Not interested	10.0
No reason given	1.2
Other reason specified: (deaths in family, hospitalization, child away at school, etc.)	18.8

TABLE B-2

EDUC: WHAT IS THE HIGHEST GRADE IN ELEMENTARY SCHOOL, HIGH SCHOOL OR COLLEGE THAT YOU FINISHED AND GOT CREDIT FOR?

	Refusal Quex	Completed Quex	Delta
Grade School or less (1st - 7th grades)	2.6%	1.3	1.3
Completed grade school (8th grade)	0.0	2.4	-2.4
Some high school (9th - 11th grades)	14.2	12.8	1.4
Completed high school (12th grade)	39.0	30.5	8.5
Some college	26.0	26.2	- .2
Completed college	11.7	12.5	- .8
More than college	6.5	14.4	-7.9

TABLE B-3

KIDGRADE: (AGRADE) IN GENERAL, WHAT KIND OF GRADES DOES YOUR CHILD --(CHILD RESPONDENT)--GET IN SCHOOL?

	Refusal Quex	Completed Quex	Delta
Excellent (Mostly A's and B's)	22.1 %	40.4	-18.3
Good (Mostly B's and C's)	28.6	42.7	-14.1
About average (Mostly C's)	48.1	9.3	39.8
Below average (Mostly C's, D's and F's)	1.3	7.6	-6.3

TABLE B-4

HAPPYKID: TAKING EVERYTHING INTO CONSIDERATION, HOW HAPPY WAS YOUR CHILDHOOD?

	Refusal Quex	Completed Quex	Delta
Very happy	31.6 %	29.8	1.8
Pretty happy	59.2	51.8	7.4
Not too happy	5.3	16.1	-10.8
Not happy at all	4.0	2.3	1.7

TABLE B-5

CLOSEFA: WHEN YOU WERE GROWING UP, HOW CLOSE WOULD YOU SAY YOU WERE TO YOUR FATHER OR TO YOUR STEP-FATHER?

	Refusal Quex	Completed Quex	Delta
Very close	36.4 %	27.9	8.5
Pretty close	41.5	40.9	.6
Not very close	18.2	27.6	-9.4
Had no father or stepfather	3.9	3.6	.3

TABLE B-6

FADRKOK: (FAOKDRNK) WHEN YOU WERE ABOUT SIXTEEN, DID YOUR FATHER APPROVE OR DISAPPROVE OF PEOPLE HAVING DRINKS CONTAINING ALCOHOL?

	Refusal Quex	Completed Quex	Delta
Approve	56.0 %	56.6	- .6
Disapprove	41.2	31.6	9.6
Did not live with father	3.0	11.8	-8.8

TABLE B-7

AGE OF RESPONDENT (COMPUTED FROM BIRTH MONTH, DAY, YEAR)

	Refusal Quex	Completed Quex	Delta
20 - 29	1.4 %	0.0	1.4
30 - 39	23.3	26.0	-2.7
40 - 49	49.8	51.0	-1.2
50 - 59	21.1	24.0	-2.9
60 and above	2.8	1.0	1.8

TABLE B-8

SERVEDRK: (OFFERDRK) DO YOU USUALLY SERVE DRINKS TO GUESTS WHO VISIT YOUR HOME?

	Refusal Quex	Completed Quex	Delta
Yes	65.0 %	70.3	-5.3
No	35.0	29.7	5.3

TABLE B-9

YOUDRINK: (DRINKNOW) DO YOU EVER DRINK? (DO YOU DRINK NOW?)

	Refusal Quex	Completed Quex	Delta
Yes	83.5 %	89.9	-6.4
No	16.5	10.1	6.4

TABLE B-10

SELFRATE: WHAT KIND OF DRINKER DO YOU CONSIDER YOURSELF TO BE?

	Refusal Quex	Completed Quex	Delta
Non-drinker	--	16.5 %	
Infrequent drinker	60.0	44.2	15.8
Moderate drinker	37.1	35.1	2.0
One who drinks quite a bit	2.9	4.2	-1.3

TABLE B-11

MISSDRK: IF YOU HAD TO GIVE UP DRINKING ALTOGETHER, HOW MUCH DO YOU THINK YOU WOULD MISS IT?

	Refusal Quex	Completed Quex	Delta
A lot	4.3 %	5.4	- 1.1
Some	7.1	17.2	-10.1
A little	23.0	23.5	- .5
Not at all	66.0	43.6	22.4
Non-drinker	--	10.2	

TABLE B-12

SEEKHELP: (FAMHELP AND OUTHELP) IF THERE WAS A DRINKING PROBLEM IN YOUR FAMILY, WOULD YOU TRY TO SOLVE THE PROBLEM WITHIN THE FAMILY, WOULD YOU SEEK OUTSIDE HELP OR ADVICE, OR WHAT WOULD YOU DO?

	Refusal Quex	Completed Quex	Delta
Solve in family	28.0 %	41.5	-13.5
Seek outside help	55.0	71.9	
Both	17.0	--	

TABLE B-13

OCSTATUS: ARE YOU CURRENTLY WORKING FULL TIME, PART TIME, RETIRED, LOOKING FOR WORK, KEEPING HOUSE, GOING TO SCHOOL OR WHAT?

	Refusal Quex	Completed Quex	Delta
Working full time	54.5 %	55.5	- 1.0
Working part time	9.1	14.6	- 5.5
Have a job, but am not at work because of temporary illness, vacation or strike	0.0	1.2	- 1.2
Unemployed, laid off, looking for work	1.3	3.0	- 1.7
Retired	3.9	.4	3.5
In School	2.6	1.0	1.6
Keeping house	27.3	23.3	4.0
Other	1.3	1.0	1.3

APPENDIX C
Questionnaire Items Used to Construct Variables

ITEMS IN FAMILY DRINKING VARIABLE

How often did your father or stepfather have drinks containing alcohol when you were about sixteen? (circle one)
    Two or more times a day
    Once a day
    Two to four times a week
    One to four times a month
    Less than once a month
    Never had alcoholic drinks

When you were about sixteen, did your mother or stepmother approve or disapprove of people having drinks containing alcohol? (circle one)
    Approved
    Disapproved
    Did not live with mother

How often did your mother or stepmother have drinks containing alcohol when you were about sixteen? (circle one)
    Two or more times a day
    Once a day
    Two to four times a week
    One to four times a month
    Less than once a month
    Never had alcoholic drinks

When you were about sixteen, how often did your parent(s) offer a drink when a visitor came to your home? (circle one)
    Always
    Sometimes
    Never

Was there ever any drinking problem in your own home when you were

growing up?
    Yes
    No

ITEMS IN FAMILY STRUCTURE VARIABLE

Power

When your family was growing up, how were decisions usually made in your family? (circle one)
    Father made the decisions
    Mother made the decisions
    Parents acted together
    Decisions were made some other way

How were decisions *usually* made about the punishment of children for misbehavior? (circle one)
    Father made the decisions
    Mother made the decisions
    Parents acted together
    Decisions were made some other way

Support

When you were growing up, how close would you say you were to your father or your stepfather? (circle one)
    Very close
    Pretty close
    Not very close
    Had no father or stepfather

When you were growing up, how close would you say you were to your mother or your stepmother? (circle one)
    Very close
    Pretty close
    Not very close
    Had no mother or stepmother

ITEMS IN PERSONALITY FACTORS THAT APPEAR IN THE DRINKING-PROBLEMS MODEL

Efficacy

"I feel that I'm a person of worth, at

least on an equal level with others." (strongly agree [SA], agree [A], disagree [D], strongly disagree [SD])

"I am able to do most things as well as other people can." (SA, A, D, SD)

"I have confidence that when I make plans I will be able to carry them out." (SA, A, D, SD)

"I usually schedule my activities." (SA, A, D, SD)

"I like to see new things and meet new people." (SA, A, D, SD)

"It is important to me that I always do the best job that I can." (SA, A, D, SD)

"Which type of job would you prefer to have: a job that required you to make many decisions, only a few decisions, no decisions at all?"

Authority

"People who question the accepted way of doing things usually just end up causing trouble." (SA, A, D, SD)

"One should always show respect to those in authority." (SA, A, D, SD)

"It generally works out best to keep on doing things the way they have been done before." (SA, A, D, SD)

"Once I've made up my mind, I seldom change it." (SA, A, D, SD)

"I tend to like people who are always right on time for everything." (SA, A, D, SD)

Achievement

"The kind of work involved in some jobs changes quite a bit from year to year... In your opinion is that... an advantage, a disadvantage, something that doesn't matter, something you never thought about?"

Which type of job would you prefer to have: a job that required you to make... many decisions, only a few decisions, no decisions at all?"

"Work is most satisfying when there are hard problems to solve." (SA, A, D, SD)

"I am often the last one to give up trying to do something." (SA, A, D, SD)

"When I work on a project I like to take charge of things." (SA, A, D, SD)

ITEMS IN DRINKING-ENVIRONMENT VARIABLE

When you get together socially with friends, how often are drinks containing alcohol served? (circle one)
    Nearly every time
    More than half the time
    Less than half the time
    Once in a while
    Never

Among the people from your neighborhood, how many would you say drink quite a bit? (circle one)
    Nearly all
    More than half
    Less than half
    Only a few

None
Don't know

Do you usually offer drinks to guests who visit your home?
Yes
No

ITEMS IN DRINKING PROBLEM VARIABLE

The amount of drinking of the respondent and the respondent's spouse was estimated by a combination of questions asking how often the respondent (and the spouse) drank beer—responses ran from several times a day to three times a year or less to never drink—how often hard liquor was drunk, and how many drinks of hard liquor were consumed. Assumptions were made about the amount of ethanol in each bottle of beer, glass of wine, or drink of hard liquor, and an estimate made on the yearly ethanol consumption. The total ounces of ethanol consumed by the spouse is the spouse's drinking variable in the adult model, and the total amount consumed by mother and father is the mother and father amount in the adolescent model.

Adult

Here are some statements about the use of alcoholic beverages. We are interested in how often you think each statement applies to you. (Circle one of the answers on each line—frequently, sometimes, never.)
I have difficulty walking straight after I have been drinking.
I have a hangover or severe headache after I have been drinking.
I fall asleep or pass out when I am drinking.
I feel very sad when I am drinking.
Without realizing what I am doing I end up drinking more than I had planned to.
I don't nurse my drinks; I toss them down pretty fast.

Adolescent

There are many occasions, places or settings in which young people may drink beer, wine, or liquor. (Please circle a response on each line to indicate how frequently you drink beer, wine, or liquor in each setting, or that you do not drink alcoholic beverages at all in that setting—never drink or don't drink in this setting, sometimes, frequently, most of the time.)
Driving around or sitting in a car at night.
Alone—when no one else is around.

As far as you know, about how many people in your grade or year in school drink alcohol at least sometimes? (circle one)
>   None of them
>   Some of them
>   Most of them
>   All of them

About how many of your close friends drink alcohol at least sometimes? (circle one)
>   None of them
>   Some of them
>   Most of them
>   All of them

APPENDIX D
A Modest Attempt at Self-Validation

Both adolescent and adult respondents were asked whether they answered the questions in the questionnaire truthfully, in an attempt to validate their responses (Table D.1). Ninety percent of the adult male respondents said they told the truth to all questions, as did 92 percent of the female adult respondents. Irish adult males were the most likely to say they had answered all the questions truthfully—8 percentage points higher than Swedish adult men. Only 5 percentage points separate Italian women from Jewish women in those saying they told the truth, Italian women being the most likely; Jewish women the least (94 percent, 89 percent).

One can get a reasonably good fix on which question was the one least often answered truthfully by simply comparing the responses on certain critical items of those who said they told the truth and those who said they did not. Those who said they told the truth all the time have lower drinking scores and lower problem scores than those who told the truth most of the time. It may well be that heavy drinkers and problem drinkers indeed report more drinking and more problems than those whose alcohol use and abuse is less heavy but still do not tell the whole truth about their drinking (Table D.2). Thus, to the extent there are falsehoods in the responses to our questions, they would lead to even sharper differentiation among the various ethnic groups. Since problem drinkers are less likely to tell the truth but more likely to still check problem-drinking behavior, and since the Irish are most likely to have drinking-problems and Jews least likely, if one takes falsehood into account the difference between the Irish and Jews would be even sharper than it is reported to be here.

Furthermore, there is no difference among Jews between those who say they told the truth all the time and those who say they told the truth most of the time on the problem-drinking questions (Table D.3). But there is enormous difference between the two Irish groups (56 standardized points).

Eighty-five percent of the adolescents report they told the truth all of the time (Table D.4). Just as among the adults, those who admit they told falsehoods report that they drink more than those who say they told the truth, leading us to suspect that while they admit more, they still have not admitted the whole truth. But there is no difference between either group of respondents and their drinking-problem scores (Table D.5). Irish young people, however, like their parents, sharply differentiate between those who say they have told the truth and those who admit that they have not on the problem-drinking scale, with the latter being 19 points higher in problem drinking than the former (Table D.6). Thus, to the extent that the self-description as truth tellers is accurate, the falsification of responses to the questionnaire would lead to a sharpening of the differences between the two extreme ethnic groups in the study.

TABLE D-1

TOLD THE TRUTH "ALL OF THE TIME"
(Adults)

Group	Percent	
	Men	Women
Irish	94	91
Italian	89	94
Jew	93	89
Swede	87	93
English	88	93

TABLE D-2

DIFFERENCES BETWEEN THOSE WHO TOLD THE TRUTH
"ALL OF THE TIME" AND "MOST OF THE TIME"
(Adults)

	All	Most
Problem scale	-.03	.29
Total Ounces	207	266

TABLE D-3

PROBLEM SCORES FOR JEWS AND IRISH
BY "TRUTH TELLING"
(Adults)

	All	Most
Irish	.10	.66
Jew	-.34	-.32

Modest Attempt at Self-Validation

TABLE D-4

TOLD THE TRUTH "ALL OF THE TIME"
(Adolescents)

Group	Percent
Irish	83
Italian	82
Jew	83
Swede	88
English	89

TABLE D-5

DIFFERENCES BETWEEN THOSE WHO TOLD THE TRUTH
"ALL OF THE TIME" AND "MOST OF THE TIME"
(Adolescents)

	All	Most
Problem Scale	.00	.00
Total Ounces	53	64

TABLE D-6

PROBLEM SCORES FOR JEWS AND IRISH
BY "TRUTH TELLING"
(Adolescents)

	All	Most
Irish	.00	-.18
Jew	-.20	-.63

130 Appendix D

Bibliography

Alba, Richard. 1976. "Social Assimilation among American Catholic National-origin Groups." *American Sociological Review* 41:1030-46.

Babbie, Earl. 1973. *Survey Research Methods.* Belmont, Calif.: Wadsworth.

Bacon, Margaret and Mary Brush Jones. 1968. *Teenage Drinking.* New York: Thomas Y. Crowell.

Bailey, Kenneth. 1978. *Methods of Social Research.* New York: The Free Press.

Bales, Robert F. 1946. "Cultural Differences in Rates of Alcoholism." *Quarterly Journal of Studies on Alcohol* 6:480-99.

———. 1962. "Attitudes toward Drinking in the Irish Culture." In *Society, Culture and Drinking Patterns,* D. Pittman and R. Snyder, eds. New York: Wiley and Sons.

Cahalan, D. 1970. *Problem Drinkers: A National Survey.* San Francisco: Jossey-Bass, Inc.

———. 1976. "Ethnoreligious Group Differences: 1974 California Drinking Survey." Berkeley: Social Research Group.

Cahalan, D., I.H. Cisin, and H.M. Crossley. 1969. *American Drinking Practices.* New Brunswick, NJ.: Rutgers Center of Alcohol Studies, Monograph No. 6.

Cahalan, D. and R. Room. 1974. *Problem Drinking among American Men.* New Brunswick, NJ.: Rutgers Center of Alcohol Studies, Monograph No. 7.

Cowley, Martin. 1978. "No Matter the Price the Drinkers Still Pay." *The Irish Times,* July 25.

das Gupta, Jyotirindra. 1975. "Ethnicity, Language Demands, and National Development in India." In *Ethnicity: Theory and Experience,* Nathan Glazer and Daniel P. Moynihan, eds. Cambridge: Harvard University Press.

Esman, Milton J. 1975. "Communal Conflict in Southeast Asia." In *Ethnicity: Theory and Experience,* Nathan Glazer and Daniel P. Moynihan, eds. Cambridge: Harvard University Press.

Gambino, Richard. 1974. *Blood of my Blood: The Dilemma of the Italian Americans.* New York: Doubleday.

Gans, Herbert. 1962. *Urban Villagers.* Glencoe, Ill: The Free Press.

Glad, D.C. 1947. "Attitudes and Experiences of American-Jewish and American-Irish Male Youth as Related to Differences in Adult Rates of Inebriety." *Quarterly Journal of Studies on Alcohol* 8:406-72.

Glazer, Nathan and Daniel P. Moynihan. 1970. *Beyond the Melting Pot.* Cambridge: The M.I.T. Press.

———. 1975. *Ethnicity: Theory and Experience.* Cambridge: Harvard University Press.

Gordon, Milton. 1964. *Assimilation in American Life: The Role of Race, Religion and National Origins.* New York: Oxford University Press.

Greeley, Andrew M. 1974. "Political Participation among Ethnic Groups in the United States: a Preliminary Reconnaissance." *American Journal of Sociology* 80:170-204.

———. 1975. "A Model for Ethnic Political Socialization." *American Journal of Political Science* 19:187-206.

———. 1977. *The American Catholic.* New York: Basic Books.

Greeley, Andrew and William McCready. 1975. "The Transmission of Cultural Heritages: The Case of the Irish and the Italians." In *Ethnicity: Theory and Experience,* Nathan Glazer and Daniel P. Moynihan, eds. Cambridge: Harvard University Press.

———. 1978. "Intimacy in Catholic Family Life." Presented at Social Science/Theology Colloquium, Barat College, Lake Forest, Ill., June 1978.

Hoffman, H., R.G. Loper, and Kammeier. 1974. "Identifying Future Alcoholics with MMPI Alcoholism Scales." *Quarterly Journal of Studies on Alcohol* 35:490.

Horowitz, Donald. 1975. "Ethnic Identity. In *Ethnicity: Theory and Experience,* Nathan Glazer and Daniel P. Moynihan, eds. Cambridge: Harvard University Press.

Human, Herbert. 1954. *Interviewing in Social Research.* Chicago: University of Chicago Press.

Isaacs, Harold. 1975. "Basic Group Identity: The Idols of the Tribe." In *Ethnicity: Theory and Experience,* Nathan Glazer and Daniel P. Moynihan, eds. Cambridge: Harvard University Press.

Jellinek, E.M. 1960. *The Disease Concept of Alcoholism.* Highland Park, N.J.: Hillhouse Press.

Jennings, M. Kent. 1971. *The Student-Parent Socialization Study.* Ann Arbor: University of Michigan Interuniversity Consortium for Political Research.

Jennings, M. Kent, and Kenneth P. Langton. 1968. "Political Socialization and the High School Civics Curriculum in the United States." *American Political Science Review,* Sept.

Jennings, M. Kent, and Richard Niemi. 1968. "The Transmission of Political Values from Parent to Child." *American Political Science Review,* March.

Kennedy, Robert E., Jr. 1973. *The Irish: Emigration, Marriage and Fertility.* Berkeley: University of California Press.

Kilson, Martin. 1975. "Blacks and Neo-Ethnicity in American Political Life." In *Ethnicity: Theory and Experience,* Nathan Glazer and Daniel P. Moynihan, eds. Cambridge: Harvard University Press.

Knupfer, G. and Room, R. 1967. "Drinking Patterns and Attitudes of Irish, Jewish and White Protestant American Men." *Quarterly Journal of Studies on Alcohol* 28:676-99.

Landes, Ruth and Mark Zborowski. 1958. "Hypotheses Concerning the Eastern European Jewish Family." In *Social Perspectives on Behavior,* Stein and Cloward, eds. Glencoe, Ill: The Free Press.

Larkin, Emmet. 1972. "A Devotional Revolution in Ireland—1850 to 1875." *American Historical Review* 77:625-52.

Lolli, G., E. Serianni, G.M., Golder, and P. Luzzato-Fegiz. 1958. "Alcohol in Italian Culture: Food and Wine in Relation to Sobriety among Italians and Italian Americans." New Brunswick, NJ.: Rutgers Center of Alcohol Studies, monograph No. 3.

Mazrui, Ali A. 1975. "Ethnic Stratification and the Military Agrarian Complex: The Uganda Case." In *Ethnicity: Theory and Experience,* Nathan Glazer and Daniel P. Moynihan, eds. Cambridge: Harvard University Press.

McCord J. and W. McCord. 1960. *Origins of Alcoholism.* Palo Alto: Stanford University Press.

McCready, William C. and A.M. Greeley. 1976. *The Ultimate Values of the American Population.* Beverly Hills: Sage Publications.

McClellan, D.C., W.N. Davis, and E. Wanner. 1972. *The Drinking Man.* New York: Free Press.

National Opinion Research Center. 1966. *The Education of Catholic Americans: The Final Report of Study 476.* A. Greeley and P. Rossi. Aldine: Chicago.

———. 1976. *The General Social Survey.* Data collected for the social science community under the direction of James A. Davis, Harvard University and Thomas Smith, National Opinion Research Center.

Novak, Michael. 1971. *The Rise of the Unmeltable Ethnics.* New York: MacMillan.

Patterson, Orlando. 1975. "Context and Choice in Ethnic Allegiance: A Theoretical Framework and Caribbean Case Study." In *Ethnicity: Theory and Experiences,* Nathan Glazer and Daniel P. Moynihan, eds. Cambridge: Harvard University Press.

———. 1978. *Ethnic Chauvinisim.* New York: Harper & Row.

Porter. 1975. "Ethnic Pluralism in Canadian Perspective." In *Ethnicity: Theory and Experience,* Nathan Glazer and Daniel P. Moynihan, eds. Cambridge: Harvard University Press.

Sadoun, R., G. Lolli and M. Silverman. 1965. *Drinking in French Culture.* New Brunswick, NJ.: Rutgers Center of Alcohol Studies.

Skolnick, J.S. 1954. "Arrest for Inebriety." *Quarterly Journal of Studies on Alcohol* 15:622-630.

Snyder, C. 1958. *Alcoholism and the Jews.* New Haven: Yale Center of Alcohol Studies.

Stein, Rita K. 1972. *Disturbed Youth and Ethnic Family Patterns.* Albany: State University of New York Press.

Steinfield, Melvin. 1970. *Cracks in the Melting Pot.* Beverly Hills: Glencoe Press.

Stivers, Richard. 1976. *A Hair of the Dog: Irish Drinking and the American Stereotype.* University Park: Pennsylvania State University Press.

Straus, R. and S.D. Bacon, 1951. *Alcoholism and Social Stability: A Study of Occupational Integration and Two Thousand and Twenty-Three Male Patients.* New Haven: Hillhouse Press.

Strauss, Murray A. 1964. "Power and Support Structure of the Family in Relation to Socialization." *Journal of Marriage and the Family,* 318-326.

Ullman, A.D. 1958. "Sociocultural Background of Alcoholism." *American Academy of Political and Social Science* 315:48-54.

Wechsler, Henry, et. al. 1970. "Religious-ethnic Differences in Alcohol Consumption." *Journal of Health and Social Behavior* 11:21-29.

Williams, Thomas R. 1959. "A Critique of the Assumptions of Survey Research." *Public Opinion Quarterly* 23 (Spring):55-62.

Wolfenstein, Martha. 1955. "Two Types of Jewish Mothers." In *Childhood and Contemporary Cultures,* Margaret Mead and Martha Wolfenstein, eds. Chicago: University of Chicago Press.

Wotrube, Thomas R. 1966. "Monetary Inducements and Mail Questionnaire Response." *Journal of Marketing Research* 3 (November):398-400.

INDEX

Acculturation, *see* ethnicity

Adolescent attitudes:
  and drinking environments, 40-45
  and drug use, 83-85
  and education, 20
  and family structure, 22-26, 74-78
  and parental drinking, 53-61, 73-78
  and peer-group influence, 54-55, 73-78
  and political values, 19-21
  future projections for, 97

Affection, 5, 12
  and alcohol use, 55
  and drug use, 84
  and family structures, 22

Alba, Richard, 16, 91

Alcoholism
  and loss to U.S. economy, 1
  consumption levels of, 1, 38, 40, 43, 56
  incipient, 3
  see also problem drinking

Assimilation, *see* ethnicity

Bacon, Margaret, 2, 3, 5, 21

Bailey, Kenneth, 105

Bales, Robert, 2, 5

Beer, 39, 43

Boys, 59-60, 73-75 *see also* men
  and drinking environments, 40-45
  and problem drinking, 59-60

Cahalan, D., 2

Cigarettes, 83
  and marijuana use, 84

Cisin, I.H., 2

Civic tolerance, *see* political values

College students, 2, 3

Conflicts, *see* political values

Cosmopolitanism, *see* political values

Crossley, H.M., 2

Cynicism, *see* political values

Das Gupta, Jyotirindra, 16

Drinking environments, 40-45, 53-61, 72-75, 96
  and drug use, 84
  and frequency of drinking, 27

Drug use, 83-89, 96
  and alcohol use, 96
  and cigarettes, 83
  and parental values, 84
  and pep pills, 83
  see also marijuana

Education
  and adolescent values, 20
  and drinking, 2
  and family structure, 26
  and political values, 20-26
  attainment of, 89-90

Efficacy, 37-38, 72-78, *see also* political values

Ego strength, *see* political values

English, 2, 3, 18-19
  and adolescent drinking, 42-44
  and alcohol use, 39-45
  and drinking environment, 41
  and problem drinking, 3

Esman, Milton, 16

Ethnicity
  and alcohol use, 37-45, 53-61, 90
  and assimilation, 15-17, 89-99
  and drug use, 84-85
  and family structure, 21-26
  and persistence, 89-92, 95-99
  and political values, 19-20
  and social class, 20-21
  models for studies of, 15-17

135

Index

Family structure, 4, 6-7
  and drinking, 53-62
  and ethnicity, 21-26
  and political values, 21-26
  and socialization, 26-27, 89-92, 95-99

Father's drinking, 54-61, 89, 97, *see also* men

Food, 5, 39

Frequency of alcohol consumption, 27, 39-45

Gallup Poll, 1

Gambino, Richard, 7

Gans, Herbert, 16

Genetic transmission, 76

German Protestants, 22

Girls, 56, 60-61, 75-77 *see also* women
  and problem drinking, 60-61
  drinking environments of, 40-55
  influence of father's drinking on, 55
  influence of mother's drinking on, 56

Glad, D.C., 2, 4

Glazer, Nathan, 16

Gordon, Milton,. 15

Grandparents
  and level of alcohol consumption, 38-39
  number born in the United States, 90-91

Greeley, Andrew, 22, 38, 99

Hoffman, H., 6

Homosexuality, 4, *see also* sexuality

Horowitz, David, 15

Human, Herbert, 104

Identity, 15, *see also* political values

Ideology, 15, 19, 20-26

Immigration, ethnic, 17

Ireland, 6

Irish, 2, 3, 6
  adolescent drinking, 42-44
  alcohol use, 37-45, 98-99
  drug use, 83-85
  ego strength, 19
  family structure, 21-26
  grandparents and consumption, 38
  parents and drinking, 37, 45, 75-78
  political values, 19-26, 98-99
  power in families, 37, 53-61
  recreation among the, 4
  support in families, 37, 53-61

Isaacs, Harold, 15, 16

Italians, 2, 3
  adolescent drinking, 42-44
  alcohol use, 37-45
  drug use, 83-85
  family structure, 21-26
  grandparents' consumption, 38
  parents' drinking, 37-45, 74-78
  political values, 19, 22-26
  power in families, 37, 53-61
  spouses' drinking, 72-78
  support in families, 37, 53-61

Jacobsen, Christian, 71

Jellinek, E.M, 2

Jennings, M. Kent, 18, 19, 22, 23

Jewish, 2, 3, 5
  adolescent drinking, 42-44
  alcohol use, 37-45
  drug use, 83-85
  family structure, 21-26
  parents' drinking, 37-45, 74-78
  political values, 19-20, 22
  power in families, 37, 53-61
  religious factor, 61
  ritual drinking, 5
  spouses' drinking, 72-78
  support in families, 37, 53-61

Jones, Mary Brush, 2, 5

Kennedy, Robert E., 6

Kilson, Martin, 16

Knupfer, G., 2, 3, 6

Landes, Ruth, 22

Langton, Kenneth, 18, 19, 22, 23

Lolli, G, 2

Loper, R.G., 6

Male power drive, 4

Manhattan Mental Health Study, 6

Marijuana, 1, 83-89
  leglization of, 83

Marriage, ethnic inter-, 91-92, see also spouse

Mazuri, Ali, 16

McClellan, D.C., 4, 73, 78

McCord, J., and W. McCord, 2, 3

McCready, William, 38, 99

Men see also boys
  and alcohol use, 72-73
  and drinking environment, 40-45
  and problem drinking, 55-59

Methodology, data collection, 28-29, 101-109

Minnesota Multiphasic Personality Inventory, 6

Mother's drinking, 5, 54, 56, 72-78, 84, 89, 97 see also women

Moynihan, Daniel, 16

National Opinion Research Center, 2-3, 16, 17, 61, 71, 83, 101-02

Neighborhood, 89, 90-91

Nicotine, see cigarettes

Niemi, Richard, 18

Nonabstainers, 3, 27, 44-45

Novak, Michael, 15

Parental education and political values, 26

Parental values
  and adolescent values, 19
  and alcohol consumption, 39-41, 53-61
  and drinking influence, 53-61
  and drug use, 84
  and ethnicity, 20-21
  and political values, 20
  and problem drinking, 73-78

Patterson, Orlando, 15, 16, 98-99

Persistence, ethnic, see ethnicity

Political values, 17-20
  and family structure, 21-26

Power, 21, 22-26, 28, 37, 53-61, 84

Problem drinking, 28, 58-62, 95
  and drug use, 84
  and ethnicity, 37-45
  and family structure, 28-29, 54-58
  and parental disapproval, 73-78
  in boys, 59-60
  in girls, 58-59
  in men, 58-59
  in women, 60
  mother's influence on, 89

Religion, 5, 27, 57, 58n, 61, 89

Room, R., 2, 3, 6

Sexuality, 5, 6

Skolnick, J.S., 2

Slavs, 3

Snyder, C., 2, 5, 57

Social class and ethnicity, 16, 20-21

Social trust, see political values

Socialization to alcohol, 26-27

Spouse's drinking, 28, 53-61, 72-68

Stein, Rita, 15, 16, 22

Stivers, Richard, 6, 78

Strauss, Murray, 2, 3, 21

Stubbornness, see political values

Support, 21, 22-26, 28, 37, 53-61, 84
Swedish
 adolescent drinking, 42-44
 alcohol use, 37-45
 drug use, 83-85
 family structure, 21-26
 parents' drinking, 37-45, 74-78
 political values, 20, 22
 power in families, 37, 53-61
 spouses' drinking, 72-78
 support in families, 37, 53-61

Tolerance, *see* political values

Ullman, A.D., 2, 28

Variance, 77-78

Wechsler, Henry, 2
Williams, Thomas, 104
Wine, 39, 43, 58n
Wolfenstein, Martha, 22
Women, 55-56, 59-60, 75 *see also* girls
 and drinking environments, 40-45
 and problem drinking, 60
Wotrube, Thomas, 103

Zborowski, Mark, 22